FAMILIES SPEAK
OUT

INTERNATIONAL PERSPECTIVES ON
FAMILIES' EXPERIENCES OF DISABILITY

Helle Mittler

Brookline Books

Library of Congress Cataloging-in-Publication Data

Mittler, Helle.
    Families speak out: international perspectives on families' experiences of disability / Helle and Peter Mittler.
        p.   cm.
    Includes bibliographical references.
    ISBN 1-57129-001-X
        1. Mentally handicapped—Family relationships. 2. Handicapped—Family relationships. I. Mittler, Peter J. II. Title.
HV3004.M58   1995
362.4'043—dc20   94-38388
                                                      CIP

Brookline Books

P.O. Box 1046
Cambridge, MA 02238-1046

TABLE OF CONTENTS

ACKNOWLEDGEMENTS

I would like to thank Victor Wahlstrom, President of the International League of Societies for Persons with Mental Handicap, 1990-1994, for giving me the unique opportunity of contributing to IYF as Co-chair of the Task Force. My thanks go to all our Task Force members for helping to collect the stories on which this book is based. My special thanks go to Peter, my husband and co-chair, for his help in making our co-chairing such an enjoyable and stimulating experience and for his support and encouragement.

Above all, I thank all the families and individual family members for their generosity in sharing with us their experiences, views and feelings.

FOREWORD

Professor Gunnar Dybwad, Brandeis University

It was the revolt of parents with children with intellectual limitations that in the middle and late 1940s brought positive, upbeat and action-oriented thinking into a rather stagnant field, all too preoccupied with the control and segregation of people whose limited capacity was seen as an acute threat to society.

The parents' campaign which sprang up simultaneously in Europe and the Americas as well as Australia and New Zealand was very successful in creating an awareness of new challenges on the part of both governments and professional groups such as in medicine, psychology, education, nursing and related fields. But once these professional groups collaborated with government agencies in developing complex systems of services toward meeting those challenges, the initiating role of the parents got lost sight of. More and more, they were seen only as recipients of services, as 'consumers' in need of guidance and assistance. However, in the 1980s, as an increasing interest in individualized planning developed, there became evident in both practice and literature a new appreciation of the positive pivotal roles played by mother and father, and also brother and sister and other relatives, in the lives of people with intellectual limitations. This "rediscovery of the family" was of particular significance in the more highly developed countries, because it was there that the combination of professionalism and bureaucracy had greatly diminished the role of parents.

One of the strengths of this book is the unusual extent of its international coverage. It provides direct verbatim statements of parents and others from such Third World countries as Jordan, Bangladesh, China and Tanzania. Many of these statements show that what these parents are expressing is often quite in tune with the latest developments in the 'advanced' ii • Familes Speak Out

countries. This is particularly evident in the key section entitled "Thinking About the Future," where, for example, a parent from Jordan and another from Tanzania reveal plans for their children's future that correspond to today's best thinking.

This is a very timely book. We are greatly indebted to Helle and Peter Mittler for this most helpful contribution to our field. And in no way do I mean to diminish my appreciation for their work when I say in conclusion that I look forward to the day in the not too distant future when we may be presented with a similarly compiled worldwide anthology of direct statements from members of People First and similar self-advocacy organizations now in existence in many countries around the world. Some of these groups in the USA have chosen the name *Speaking for Ourselves*, and indeed these voices, too, need our thoughtful attention.

October 1994

Brandeis University
Waltham, Massachusetts, USA

PREFACE

Professor Peter Mittler, Co-chair ILSMH Task Force

This book is a contribution to the United Nations International Year of the Family. It arises from the work of a Task Force established by the International League of Societies for Persons with Mental Handicap to ensure that the situation of families worldwide who have a relative with a mental handicap should be made known in the hope that their needs might be better met in the future than in the past.

The United Nations* identified the following objectives for IYF:

- Increase awareness of family issues among governments as well as in the private sector
- Highlight the importance of families
- Increase understanding of their functions and problems
- Promote knowledge of the economic, social and demographic processes affecting families and their members
- Focus attention on the rights and responsibilities of all family members
- Strengthen national institutions to formulate, implement and monitor policies in respect of families
- Stimulate efforts to respond to problems affecting and affected by the situation of families
- Enhance the effectiveness of local, regional and national efforts to carry out specific programs concerning families by generating new activities and strengthening existing ones
- Improve collaboration among national and international non-governmental organizations in support of multi-sectorial activities

---

* United Nations (1991) 1994 *International Year of the Family: Building the Smallest Democracy at the Heart of Society.* Vienna: United Nations

- Build upon the results of international activities concerning women, children, youth, the aged, *the disabled*, as well as other major events of concern to the family or its individual members.

THE INTERNATIONAL LEAGUE OF SOCIETIES FOR PERSONS WITH MENTAL HANDICAP

ILSMH was founded in 1962 and now has 150 member societies in nearly 100 countries. Almost all the work is done on a voluntary basis, with the support of a very small secretariat in Brussels.

Four fundamental principles underlie all aspects of the League's work. These are INCLUSION, FULL CITIZENSHIP, SELF-DETERMINATION, and FAMILY SUPPORT.

The League works at a variety of levels:

- Encouraging the establishment and development of national and local societies in all countries, especially developing countries and countries where services are lacking
- Publishing and disseminating reports on developments worldwide, as well as occasional newsletters and information sheets
- Setting up committees, working parties and task forces on specific areas of need, with a view to sharing ideas and experiences and disseminating results and recommendations worldwide
- Lobbying United Nations and other international organizations to ensure that issues concerned with people with mental handicap and their families are included in policies and discussions on social and humanitarian affairs
- Lobbying national governments, especially in relation to human rights and abuse issues

ILSMH AND IYF

The League welcomed the inclusion of disability issues in the original UN/IYF objectives but feared that the needs of families with a disabled member could easily be overlooked. Furthermore, we felt that the declaration of 1994 as the International Year of the Family provided an excellent opportunity to make the fullest possible use of the year to benefit such families all over the world. It was therefore necessary to find a means of informing and encouraging our members to take advantage of this opportunity.

This was the background to the establishment of the League's IYF Task Force in 1992. Helle Mittler and I were appointed as co-chairpersons. One mother and one father were appointed from each of the main regions of the world — Africa, Asia, the Arab region, Australasia, North America, South America and Europe — as well as the chairs of the Leagues's existing committees on the Family and on Brothers and Sisters.

The names of the Task Force members are listed at the end of this Preface. Some members were already active and influential in their own countries as well as internationally. For others, it was their first experience of international work or of travelling outside their own country.

Unfortunately, it proved impossible to find a father from Latin America. Ill health and major family commitments also made it difficult for some members to contribute to the Task Force to the extent that they would have wished. But despite these and other obstacles (mainly financial), members of the Task Force worked hard and successfully to meet their objectives.

AIMS OF THE TASK FORCE

A small grant from the United Nations IYF Voluntary Fund helped to make it possible to hold our first meeting in February 1993. At that meeting, we agreed on a number of general aims and specific objectives for the Task Force:

1. Ensure that disability issues are included in IYF at the international and regional levels and in every country where there are ILSMH member societies.
2. Raise public awareness of the strengths and needs of families with a member who has a mental handicap in order to stimulate action to improve the quality of life of families.
3. Clarify variations in the experience of families in different countries and regions, disabled members at different life stages and with a range of needs arising from profound levels of disability or from behavior which is difficult to manage.

OBJECTIVES OF THE TASK FORCE

1. Collect information on the situation of families with a member with a mental handicap in regions and countries with ILSMH member societies in order to obtain a clearer picture of the needs of families. The first results of this objective form the substance of this book.
2. Establish a mechanism for information sharing between countries and regions.
3. Collect examples of good practice in actions and initiatives to improve the quality of life of families with a disabled member with a view to increasing information about the range of options for families.
4. Keep member societies informed about the existence of IYF national coordinating committees in their countries, so that they can ensure that the interests of families with a disabled

member are represented.

5. Initiate actions to increase public understanding of the strengths and needs of families.
6. Write to national and local government agencies in order to represent the interests of families.
7. Initiate actions that will empower families.

LEARNING MESSAGES

Task Force members also agreed on a set of principles which expressed the aims and philosophy of the Task Force. These *Learning Messages* were widely disseminated not only within ILSMH but also to the international community, including the main UN organizations and other national and international non-governmental organizations.

1. All people are valued members of the world community
2. People with a mental handicap and their families are equal, participating members of their communities. They have the same rights as other citizens to:
   • participation in decisions which affect their lives
   • diversity of choice for housing, education, work, recreation and leisure
   • equity and justice
   • empowerment to take their full place in the community
   • dignity and privacy in all aspects of their lives
3. We are all likely to experience disability at some time in our lives either personally or through members of our family and community.
4. Society can add to or lessen disability.
5. People with mental handicap have abilities. They can and do contribute to society, but their ability to do so is often underestimated.
6. People with a disability have a right to be consulted, to make informed choices and to exercise control in planning their own lives.

7. People with a disability and their families and carers have an important contribution to make to policy development, planning and delivery of services and to training about disability issues.
8. It is normal to be different.
9. People with a disability have useful knowledge about their own needs, strengths and abilities.
10. Families with a member who has a disability have knowledge about their own needs, strengths and abilities.
11. Families need information.
12. Support for families with a member who has a disability makes economic sense.
13. Definitions of the family must reflect the wide range of arrangements and forms found in society.
14. Usually it is in the best interests of the family member with a disability to remain in the family environment at least during childhood. Families require practical support in order to fulfill this role. State exploitation of families must be avoided.
15. The interests, safety and welfare of the person with a disability must always be safeguarded.
16. In two-parent families, the task of caring for a family member with a disability should as far as possible be shared by both parents. Fathers and mothers both have a vital role in creating a beneficial family environment. Both can make a valuable contribution to the functioning of supportive organizations and where possible should be actively involved in those organizations.

OUTCOMES OF THE TASK FORCE

The Task Force met for a second time in February 1994 in order to review progress and decide on tasks to be accomplished for the rest of the year. One of the main aims of this meeting was to undertake detailed planning on how to present key issues arising out of the work of the Task Force to the 11th World Congress of ILSMH, due to take place in New Delhi, India in November 1994.

1. Members of the Task Force have worked to make contact with national governments in their region. They were particularly concerned to know whether governments had established a national coordinating committee for IYF, as strongly recommended by the United Nations and, if so, whether the interests of families with a disabled relative in general and one with a mental handicap in particular were represented.

Some countries replied immediately in the affirmative. In several other cases, the enquiry itself, duly backed up by the national society, led either to the addition of disability issues to the plan of IYF activities or to the appointment of one or more representatives of disability organizations. Some members of the Task Force were themselves appointed members of the national IYF Coordinating Committee for their country (Australia, Jordan, Lebanon), and others have made a strong impact on national developments in other ways.

A number of countries identified an IYF Focal Point, usually a government department but sometimes a voluntary organization. Current lists of such agencies are held by the IYF Secretariat at the United Nations Office in Vienna, Austria. Members of the Task Force informed ILSMH member societies about these contacts and planned activities and encouraged them to get in touch with these organizations in order to ensure that disability and mental handicap issues were included.

In June 1994, the following countries reported that they had an IYF coordinating committee with mental handicap representation: Australia, Austria, Bangladesh, China, Estonia, France, Germany, Hong Kong, Iceland, Israel, Jordan, Kenya, Lebanon, Luxemburg, Mexico, New Zealand, Nigeria, Portugal, Spain. The numbers should now be much larger.

2. Examples of good practice in supporting families have been collected by Task Force members, but more have still to come.

We are hoping to publish these separately.

3. A number of publications have been commissioned and produced directly bearing on IYF.

a) The United Nations commissioned us to write *Families and Disability*, one of a series of IYF Occasional Papers prepared specifically on IYF and the only one dealing with disability (available from the IYF Secretariat of the United Nations Office in Vienna, Austria).

b) We have edited a collection of articles under the title *Innovations in Family Support*, to be published later in 1994 by Lisieux Hall Press in Chorley, Lancashire, UK.

c) Short summaries of the work of the IYF Task Force have been published in the UN and UNESCO Newsletters.

d) We have given papers on the work of the IYF Task Force and on issues concerned with families who have a relative with a mental handicap at international conferences in Turkey, Iceland, Ireland and Spain.

4. In addition to the extracts from the Family Stories that follow, we hope to edit and publish a selection of the complete Family Stories in order to disseminate the information collected by the Task Force on the situation facing families in all regions of the world. We also plan to publish Examples of Good Practice in Supporting Families, collected by members of the Task Force.

August 1994
University of Manchester

MEMBERS, ILSMH INTERNATIONAL YEAR OF THE FAMILY TASK FORCE

CO-CHAIRS
Professor Peter Mittler, Manchester, England
Mrs. Helle Mittler, Manchester, England

AFRICA
Mme. Helene Haddad, Abidjan, Cote d'Ivoire
Mr. D.B.N. Marandu, Moshi, Tanzania

ARAB REGION
Dr. Moussa Charrafedine, Beirut, Lebanon
Mrs. Ghuson Kareh, Amman, Jordan

ASIA
Mrs. K.P. Gayatheri Setti, Mysore, India
Mr. Ong Ping Sam, Singapore

NORTH AMERICA
Dr. Bud Fredericks, Monmouth, Oregon, USA
Mrs. Jo Dickey, Vancouver, Canada

SOUTH AMERICA
Mrs. Gare de Zaldo, Mexico City, Mexico

AUSTRALASIA
Mrs. Gillian Deane, Wellington, New Zealand
Mr. Stan Kelly, Sydney, Australia

EUROPE
Mrs. Ingrid Korner, Hamburg, Germany
M. Raymond Neuville, La Hume, France
Mrs. Pauline Fairbrother, London, England (Chair, ILSMH Families Committee)
Mme. Therese Kempeneers-Foulon, Brussels, Belgium (Chair, ILSMH Brothers and Sisters Committee)

EX OFFICIO
Mr. Victor Wahlstrom, President, ILSMH
Mme. Paule Renoir, Administrative Director, ILSMH

INTRODUCTION

1994 was the United Nations International Year of the Family. The International League of Societies for Persons with Mental Handicap was determined that the views and needs of families with members with learning disabilities should be heard during the International Year.

To this end, the International Task Force established by ILSMH undertook to collect stories from families with a member with learning disabilities from all major regions of the world.

The purpose of the stories was to bring to public attention the current situation of families with a member with learning disabilities world wide.

A lot has been written already about disability and about learning disabilities. Most of this is in the form of reports of research studies which look at particular issues, and are specific to a particular country or culture. Only a few cross-cultural studies exist (e.g., Gartner, Lipsky and Turnbull 1991; Mittler, Mittler & McConachie 1986; Mittler & Mittler, 1994).

We felt that real stories would bring the experience of families to life and that through them families could speak directly not only to people who were already in contact with disabled people and involved in the disability field but to everyone. A few parents and other family members have written about their experiences on an individual basis. There are now also a number of collections of family stories in North America and Australia. But we believe the IYF Task Force collection of family stories is the first collection of such family experiences world wide.

Each member of the Task Force was asked to collect at least six stories from their region. The stories were to include families:

- in both urban and rural areas
- from different socioeconomic groups
- with a relative at different stages of life:
  - preschool age
  - school age
  - young adults or older.
- with a profoundly or multiply handicapped member
- with a member with emotional difficulties and/or challenging behavior.

We sketched an outline for Task Force members to use when they met with families willing to share their story, and the main topics are represented by the various sections in this book. We were also anxious to ensure protection for families who might share sensitive material with us. We therefore asked our members to ensure that all families were given a real choice as to whether they wished to take part and, if so, whether they wished their real identity to be known or not.

The 80 stories we collected are not fully representative. There is perhaps a preponderance of stories from families in Asia and the Middle East. Australasia, North America and Europe are adequately represented. There are fewer stories from Africa and fewest of all from South America.

The stories are mainly from middle-class, urban families, though a significant minority are from poor or rural areas. The members with learning disabilities mostly would be described as having moderate impairments, though an important number present profound, multiple or progressive conditions. Family members with Down Syndrome formed the largest single group in relation to the type of disability mentioned. Disabled children and adults were fairly equally represented, though there were few preschool children and few adults over 45 years.

The stories therefore cover a very wide spectrum. They are drawn from different cultures and from areas with striking differences of access to services. In Europe, Australasia and North America, services exist to support disabled people and their families from birth throughout the life cycle. The services may vary greatly in range and quality depending on the responsible authority. They may not adequately meet the needs of all families or of individual family members. They do, however, exist and can be built upon.

In many parts of Asia, Africa and South America, very few services exist. Those that do are often set up by voluntary agencies, often founded and funded by parents themselves. They are usually available only in urban areas and reach few poor families.

Attitudes to disability and to learning disabilities vary. These relate to many factors. There are some cultural differences of belief, but usually within each culture there is a wide range of attitude.

There are, of course, cultural differences in convention and, perhaps most strikingly, in gender roles. For example, in Asia, doctors often inform only the father or a male family member when a disability is diagnosed and leave him to tell the mother.

However, there seem to be greater similarities than differences in families' experiences. Many experiences are universal or almost so. It also seems clear that experiences do not only relate to the family's own resources and strengths. What is crucial is not only the availability of services but the social context in which they live, the social attitudes they encounter and, above all, whether they have a supportive social network.

Some of the family stories, those of families in the later stages of the life cycle, demonstrate remarkably their journey from trauma to strength and achievement. They tell us not only about the stresses and difficulties that they contend with but equally importantly the gains, benefits and joys that the experience of living with and caring for a family member with learning disabilities can bring. They richly demonstrate the resourcefulness, creativity and fighting spirit of the families themselves.

They do not, however, allow any room for complacency. Families have much to say about the inadequacies of social systems that exist and the innumerable ways in which they discriminate against disabled people and their families. The vast majority of families with members with learning disabilities have no access at all to family support systems.

The challenge of the future is how to reduce the tremendous inequalities that still exist: between able-bodied and disabled people and between disabled people with means and those without. The stories illustrate how inequalities experienced by disabled people and their families interact with other inequalities relating to class, race, gender, age and sexuality.

This book is a selection of what family members say about a number of key topics.

• the experience of being told that their child has a learning disability
• trying to get accurate information and practical advice
• the reactions of others
• contact with professionals
• positive and negative effects on family members

These are themes that recur in almost all the stories. Although the stories describe the family experience, it is individual voices that speak to us. Most often it is the voice of the mother, who most commonly undertakes the main caring responsibility. Sometimes it is the voice of fathers and occasionally the voice of a brother or sister. The voice of the disabled family member is only heard rarely and sometimes indirectly.

The families who told their stories were generous in the honesty, openness and frankness with which they shared their experiences and their feelings. They were motivated by the desire to increase public understanding about learning disabilities and the experiences of families with a disabled member. Their stories show how their experience is affected by the attitudes and responses of the communities in which they live.

They almost unanimously hold the view that public education about disability issues is among the highest priorities in improving the lives of disabled people and their families.

This book is their contribution to this process.

REFERENCES

Gartner, A., Lipsky, D. and Turnbull, A. (1991) *Supporting Families with a Child with a Disability: An International Outlook*. Baltimore, MD.: Paul H. Brookes.

Mittler, P., Mittler, H. and McConachie, H. (1986) *Working Together: Guidelines for Collaboration between Professionals and Parents of Children and Young People with Disabilities*. Guides to Special Education No. 2. Paris: UNESCO.

Mittler, P. and Mittler, H. (1994a) *Families and Disability*. IYF Occasional Paper No. 10. Vienna: United Nations

Mittler, P. and Mittler, H. (eds) (1994b) *Innovations in Family Support*. Chorley, Lancs.: Lisieux Hall Press (in press)

FINDING OUT

The experience of families in learning about the disability of their child or adult member varied a great deal. There are many different causes, genetic or congenital, or the result of illness, accident or war. Learning about the disability presented a common difficulty: it often took months or even years to obtain accurate information. Nor was this dependent on the socioeconomic status of families: it was equally true for families with money, a high level of education and even some medical knowledge. It also seems a common experience, whether parents are aware of "something wrong" or not.

Of course, some disabilities, most commonly Down Syndrome, were often diagnosed at birth.

The parents were very shocked when the hospital staff told them at the time of the birth that Siu Lun had Down Syndrome and would be mentally handicapped. "We just could not accept it."

Family Pang, Hong Kong

Mother was only told after one month that her baby had Down Syndrome; she had noticed his face was "strange" but did not know why. She was "Very shocked!" The doctor who told her explained that babies with Down Syndrome are either severely, moderately or mildly handicapped and also tried to explain about causes, but mother did not take this in at the time. "Doctor should have told me much more!"

Family Leung, Hong Kong

When Gaku was born he had a low birth weight but developed normally for 4 months. At 4 months he caught a cold and started having a series of severe convulsions. After this he became a poor feeder and did not gain weight, and his parents were very shocked and worried.

The first doctor they approached reassured them that Gaku would be all right; he did not understand the problem and advised them to seek specialist advice. Parents took him to a private mental hospital. The psychiatrist gave Gaku an EEG (electroencephalogram) but could find "no problem". Gaku's convulsions occurred daily. His parents remained extremely worried, anxious and distressed.

They then approached the Tokyo Government Hospital. There the 83 pediatrician discovered some "slight" problems with the EEG and prescribed anti-convulsant medication, but this failed to control the epilepsy. Gaku's seizures continued. They were advised to "accept" the situation. "We had already accepted the situation! We wanted to know what we could do for the best: it was just a philosophical lecture. They had no skill in diagnosis and we were given no adequate information."

Family Ryo, Japan

They approached religious friends, doctors, pediatricians, a neurologist and a psychiatrist. In all, the process of seeking a diagnosis took two to three years. When Abrare was nearly five years old they were told, "During the operation [a Caesarean birth], lack of oxygen damaged the baby's brain cells. Abrare is mentally retarded." Parents were advised that there was no medical treatment.

Family Chowdhury, Bangladesh

S.B. Salam knew nothing about disability when Rumana was born. She thought Rumana was a little uglier than her brothers but thought this might have been due to the effect of the war and the worry during the pregnancy which might have affected the baby.

When Rumana was four years old, S.B. Salam's sister visited the family from her home in the United States. She had seen children with Down Syndrome. She contacted another sister who was a pediatrician. The latter advised Shaher Banu to have Rumana's hearing assessed. The audiologist first mentioned Down Syndrome to Rumana's parents. They went to Calcutta to have a chromosome test, which was positive. They were very shocked.

Family Salam, Bangladesh

Mother did not know about Eu Jin's diagnosis from her doctor. She was very upset about the disability initially. At first she tried to find a cure but soon accepted the fact that there was none. It did not take the parents too long before they coped with the birth of Eu Jin. As there was no institutional help where they lived, mother wrote many letters to institutions for the intellectually disabled in the United Kingdom, the United States and Australia for an understanding of her child's disability and how she could help him.

Family Lim, Singapore

Mother was told that the baby cried only after nasopharyngeal suction. He was treated in an incubator for 2 days. Parents noticed a delay in walking when he was 16 months old. They took him to a State Hospital where he was examined by the head of Pediatrics. He told them that their son would be developmentally delayed and advised them against taking him to a mental hospital. At two years he was taken to the All India Institute of Speech and Hearing (AIISH). There again he was diagnosed as being mentally retarded. The pediatrician told them harshly that it was no use and a waste of time to bring their child to the Institute and they should keep him inside the home! This was the moment the parents became shocked and depressed; mother virtually started crying as they went back home.

Family Setty, India

Parents noticed Mukund's disability from birth by observing that his milestones were all delayed. They consulted all the well-known pediatricians, neurologists, pediatric neurologists, audiologists, psychiatrists and psychologists. None of them could advise or counsel them "properly".

Family Venugopal, India

During this time my son Walid was studying in the University. In the mornings he was assisting a pediatrician and then a pharmacist to help pay for his college expenses. He suggested I take Fatima to the private pediatrician he worked for. After the doctor examined Fatima, he asked Walid to take me downstairs to the pharmacy to get the medication. I understood that the doctor wanted to see Walid in private. My son was left with Fatima and the doctor. He never told me what the doctor told him, and I never confronted him about it because I knew my daughter would be ill according to the other pediatrician. Walid was angry and nervous for many months.

Of course Fatima had to be hospitalized and treated for the jaundice. The doctors needed to take a blood sample from her. Five different members of staff probed around in her arm with a needle trying to find a vein. I thought my baby was being tortured. I felt so weak and worried that I sat out in the corridor in a chair and started to cry. One of the pediatricians saw me and I told him what was happening to Fatima. He comforted me and told me he would handle it himself. He found a vein in her neck and took the sample. There were very few good doctors. The first year of Fatima's life was spent mostly in the hospital. She was very weak and ill. I would hear doctors saying things like "This is a Mongolian child." To me Mongolian meant merely jaundice. I didn't understand either term.

Family from Jordan

When I awoke I was told that I had a baby boy, but the faces around me were odd. The nurses came to my room and asked me to call my husband because the hospital needed to see him in person. I explained to her that I could give any information she needed, but she insisted on speaking with my husband. I phoned my husband, but he sent my mother instead to answer the nurse's questions. I found out later that he was told immediately that his son was Down Syndrome, had a condition in which there is no opening for the stool to pass, and needed urgent surgery... My husband told me later that the first pediatrician to speak with him after examining the baby had told him that this baby had many deformities and in a few hours "He will swell and die." This was why he withdrew from making any decisions about the situation, because he couldn't deal with it.

Family Ali, Jordan

When Akrima was 9 months old, he touched a heater. His hand was burned very badly, but Akrima didn't feel it. He didn't cry even once. I took him to the doctor and had some tests done, a hearing test, EEG, etc. I was told there was nothing wrong with Akrima physically.

Akrima was delayed in walking, not learning until he was 2 years old. He spoke a few words at the age of two, but after that his language started to deteriorate. Again I went to the doctor to find out why he had a language loss. They tested his hearing and I was again told that there was nothing wrong with my child, that he would learn as he grows.

Family Sarayra, Jordan

Barbara knew from the day that Lynne was born that there was something wrong. The baby was "floppy". Like so many mothers before and since, she was told that by the "experts" that she was imagining things... At 3 years old Lynne was finally diagnosed as having Smith-Lenli-Opitz Syndrome.

Lynne's Family, UK

What followed was an Odyssey throughout medical practice.
Family Thurnes, Germany

Craig's cerebral palsy was diagnosed when he was four months old. It was only due to my mother persisting that there was something wrong with him.
Craig's Family, Australia

SHARING

*Many families experienced difficulty in talking to
each other and sharing their feelings about the disability of their child. Where they were able to do
so, this was a source of strength.*

Initially, the diagnosis of Down Syndrome was made at birth.
The doctor told the father alone, as is customary in Asia. He
was deeply shocked and told no one for two weeks. After this
he shared his concern with his father, Song senior, who could
not believe the news at first. He was very shocked. He could
not understand it. The father only told his wife a month after
the birth. She was also extremely upset and wept.

Family Song, China

His mother tried to stimulate Ju Hun and to help him learn by
herself. His father offered her no support; he went fishing when
he had time away from work. She felt that she accepted the
fact that Ju Hun had a disability, but her husband found this
much harder; did not accept it and said Ju Hun would become all right gradually.

Three or four years ago she learned that a distant relative
in her husband's family also has Down Syndrome. Her husband knew of this and her mother-in-law thought Ju Hun was
another child "like that". No one told her about this. She thinks
it was deliberately kept secret, perhaps because the family
thought it would not help in any way.

Family Ha, Korea

On his return home (after he was hospitalized because of a high fever), Lee Eun's physical health was poor. She took the baby for regular checks at the hospital but was told nothing by the doctors. She knew nothing about disability.

Lee Eun's milestones were delayed, but she was not particularly worried about this and placed her faith in the doctors who were looking after him. Lee Eun did not eat well, and she spent most of the morning trying to feed him.

His walking was several months delayed and his speech was one year delayed. However she remained confident that in spite of the delay he would eventually be all right.

Only after he had started school, when he was ten years old, did Sin-Myong Yang learn from her husband that the doctors had told him when Lee Eun was a baby that he would never be "normal"! She expressed no resentment about his withholding this information from her. She understood that it was because of his great love for her that he wanted to shield her from this painful knowledge. Only when he saw how desperately she was struggling to help her son to develop and learn was he able to share the fact of their child's disability with her. He had shared it with no one else.

Family Yang, Korea

Our family is not an ordinary family. My older brother is mentally retarded. My parents were both teachers but had a poor understanding of their son. I was the youngest of six and I did not agree with how my parents reacted to the situation. When my son had epilepsy I remembered that situation, so I wrote a long letter explaining the situation to my parents.

We are usually open to family and friends and talk about our son, so we have a good situation.

Family Ryo, Japan

Sharing feelings is not easy in Bangladesh.

Family Chowdhury, Bangladesh

His wife was very worried... She cried a lot at night; could not sleep and suffered from B-complex deficiency. She did not share her worries with her husband.

Family Hossain, Bangladesh

I was told that my son was Mongoloid. I had never heard that term before, but they explained what it meant. They told me to tell my wife when her fever was better, but I didn't tell her.

Family Eed, Jordan

FIRST REACTIONS

Some parents were the first to notice that their child was not developing normally and sought expert advice. Often, parents were hopeful that even when their child's milestones were delayed they would eventually be all right. Except for parents who had known for a considerable time that something was wrong and felt relief when they were told of their child's condition, the more common initial reactions were ones of shock and upset.

My initial reaction was that of shock and disbelief that Saed is my son. I still find it difficult to deal with the problem. However, his father is more accepting.

Family Itani, Lebanon

We were first made aware of Fadi's disability during early childhood. I [Mother] always doubted that there was anything wrong, even though the doctors noticed slight psychomotor dysfunction, and I was not convinced until Fadi was 4 years old.

Family Saleh, Jordan

He was all wrapped up and looked very beautiful, so I didn't suspect that there was anything wrong with him. That morning the doctors came into my room for morning rounds. I asked one of them to explain in detail about my baby's health. I told them that I worked in special education so I was strong enough to understand and cope with the condition of my son and help him. The doctor told me that my son had Down

Syndrome and needed urgent surgery that had to be approved by his father... I didn't cry. I was too stunned... My husband came in for the first time since I had given birth and told me that we had to accept the fact that the baby had Down Syndrome:

"You are the one who loves those children and has a strong desire to work with them. Don't you bring home stories of what they do every day? There you go, this is the result of your work!"

I tried hard to convince him that my work had nothing to do with having a Down Syndrome child, but it was hopeless.

Family Ali, Jordan

The family's initial reaction was one of great tragic shock. It was very frustrating, and we felt there was a very big problem which is very difficult to face and needs a lot of energy, sacrifice and cooperation.

Family Osseiran, Jordan

Mother continued to worry and at 4 months took Ju Hun to the hospital. The doctors looked at the marks on Ju Hun's hands and advised her to take him to a larger hospital which had facilities to do chromosome tests. Here the doctors told them that Ju Hun had Down Syndrome. Both parents had gone together, and they felt that "all of a sudden Heaven broke down" on them.

Family Ha, Korea

We went for a genetic counseling session and learned that Eu Jin having Down Syndrome was an accident. We were relieved to find that it was not hereditary.

Family Lim, Singapore

The doctor said Susan was a Mongol and she is slow in everything. I don't understand what Mongol means. My mother and I thought that Susan is just like any other baby... I felt I was fated to have this baby.

Family Chan, Singapore

At first all the family found it hard to accept. The grandfather took the initiative in consulting many experts. They took Zhijia to have several assessments. They searched for a reason for what had happened. Was it due to the x-ray that his mother had during pregnancy? However, the diagnosis was always confirmed and they were given no help or advice.

"We had to accept it, but we were very sad and upset."

Family Song, China

Monti's development caused no particular anxiety in her early years. Her physical development was normal and her language seemed normal. It was the outstripping of Monti by her two younger brothers that first alerted her parents to the fear that something was wrong... Their twin sons were moved up into higher classes at school, but Monti could recognize no letters even by the time she was 10 years old... The teacher told them: "Your daughter is mentally handicapped. She has no brilliant career in her brain. She does not behave normally. Please take her away!"

Jowaherul and Momotaj were deeply upset.

Family Mamun, Bangladesh

Her parents, Christine and Val, found the degenerative nature of Rett's Syndrome difficult to understand as Joyce lost skills after gaining them, began to take multiple seizures and cried a lot. After a second opinion Joyce was diagnosed as having Rett's Syndrome. Christine continued her story, "It was like, Wow! We have a name — something to go on. I started reading about the syndrome and watched the videos and joined the National Association. I could relate to the literature as every item was similar to Joyce."

Family Morrison, New Zealand

Some members of the family do not know about Uncle Mervin.

Maori family, New Zealand

The parents at first were mystified, terrified and bewildered and thought their child was bewitched.

Family Mlaki, Tanzania

We were totally mentally upset. Abrare's mother became depressed and used to forget everything. Over time we learned to accept it as our misfortune.

Family Chowdhury, Bangladesh

We felt very lost and had no direction in looking for help.

Family Lee, Singapore

They took their time explaining about Mongoloid, chromosomes and developmental delays. I didn't hear a word that was said because I started to scream and ran out of the room. They gave me a sedative and left me to sleep for an hour. I was 22 years old at the time. They told me that they had diagnosed Ra'ad at birth and it was time that I should know. They said they would help me with Ra'ad's disability, but I refused to listen and started to see other doctors. Until he was 6 months old I couldn't believe that he was handicapped.

Family Eed, Jordan

My first two years I felt my life was finished. My smile left me forever... My life was full of horror. [Mother of a child with self-injurious behavior]

Family Saleh, Jordan

I remember saying to the doctor not long after David was born that there was no way that I could cope with a retarded child.

David's Family, Australia

When she [mother] was first told, all she could think of was "She will never have a wedding!" She said this to Mick [father], and he just put his arms around her and held her tight.

Lynne's Family, UK

It was so unexpected. It was a tremendous shock, just as if our happiness was going to be taken away from us, as if our life would change as a whole, entirely.

Family Oleffe, Belgium

WANTING TO KNOW

*Families want information and often spend years
before they find specialists who can give them an
explanation and, even more importantly, advice.
Parents and other relatives want, above all, to know
what they need to do to help their child or adult
relative to develop and to make progress.*

I would have been happy if anyone had told me about the
actual problems and the right approach.

Family Yashivim, India

As the doctor was talking to me shortly after her birth about a
"mutation," and the geneticist later used the word Mongolism
and Down Syndrome, I automatically took the traditional view:
Frederica was born as a handicapped child. It was at this time
that my own handicap came into being with full force, a condition described by so many fathers and mothers. Guilt, a
broken vision of the future; questions about the meaning of
life; death wishes; questions about why — was this the child
of our dreams?

My own handicap manifested itself in a certain emotional
liability and a strong restriction of my mental as well as physical space. It was barely possible for me to develop any thoughts
which were separate from my handicapped daughter. I often
went round and round in a circle. In the first weeks I hardly
dared go outside with the pram. I was not the proud mother

full of hope and expectation for her child, and I was afraid of the question "Is everything OK?" Before the birth I had planned to continue to work part time, but this no longer seemed possible, although I had a good babysitter for my first child. "A mother who has a handicapped child cannot work. She has to be there completely for her handicapped child." I accepted all this well-meaning advice. I soaked in all the information I could from books, and in those first weeks I believed all that I read.

Family Korner, Germany

Knowing the cause was a great release. Others seem more able to understand if you can explain.

Family Deane, New Zealand

What could have been helpful is perhaps the family could have been told about Dhanesh's condition once the doctor had diagnosed him at birth. Apparently the doctor had kept it confidential and did not want to tell their parents about Dhanesh's intellectual disability. The doctor advised them to go to the Novena Church to pray instead.

Family Acuthan, Singapore

If the gynecologists had advised the parents properly in early pregnancy about the effect of measles on the baby, the parents would have taken precautions and avoided the birth of a handicapped child.

Family Basavaraj, India

The doctor explained about Down Syndrome. He told the parents to prepare for the fact that even when he became an adult Ju Hun might not be able to live independently or be continent. He gave the parents no advice.

Family Ha, Korea

She [mother] feels it would be better if there were more information in teaching parents from the very beginning to plan for the child's future.

Family Chan, Singapore

SOCIAL ATTITUDES

Some families comment that social attitudes have improved, but many families continue to experience stressful and distressing negative attitudes toward their relative's disability and toward themselves.

The majority of neighbors and local people see the whole issue as a curse from God.

Family Marandu, Tanzania

Some years ago society did not pay enough attention to people with disabilities, but now the government is becoming more concerned.

Family Song, China

Later, when I came back to work, I was very hesitant to talk to the new colleagues because I was afraid they would leave work. Most were newly married and three were pregnant. There is a superstition in our area: if a mother is pregnant, and she loves someone and looks at him, the baby will look like him because the eye transfers attributes to the fetus. This superstition is still alive today.

Family Ali, Jordan

When I came back to tell the family about what the doctors had told me, they attacked me badly, accusing me of ruining the family's reputation by saying that my children were mentally handicapped like their father. These problems lasted for months. I discovered that my mother-in-law knew about my husband's condition but kept it from my family.

Family Abdel-Kader Ayesh, Jordan

I feel people don't really accept us but they tolerate and humor us to a degree. I feel people are polite to us only because they have a duty socially to be that way; they don't like our company.

Family Sarayra, Jordan

One day I will write a story about my daughter. I will tell people that they are hard. Their pitying looks make me fall apart inside. I interact with people as if I am above them. I force myself and my daughter on society, and at the end of the day I collapse. I am not really that strong but just trying to hold myself together. When I visit the institutional workers in Jordan I feel that if I had a cat I wouldn't leave it in the care of those who work there, not even the expensive private ones.

Family Saleh, Jordan

My husband and I accepted Ra'ad's condition, but the neighbors and other people around us did not accept him but attacked us. They considered his birth as bad luck and that we deserved the condition of our son. My mother-in-law told me that Ra'ad is not a man and that I would have to have another brother for Jerias. She did not want Jerias to be the only son.

Family Eed, Jordan

The neighbors cautioned their children to keep away from Jacqueline because she is "violent and quarrelsome".

Family Maro, Tanzania

We were deprived of a proper social life. No one could tolerate us visiting them.

Family Sarayra, Jordan

Sometimes Mrs. Ng recalled incidents when they went out; people might just stare at them and nudge their friends to take a look at Leslie, as he has difficulty in talking and uses gestures to communicate with his parents.

Family Ng, Singapore

In 1977 the prospects and circumstances for people with Down Syndrome were depicted in a thoroughly negative manner. This infected me also with a negative picture of Frederica, so that I accepted the general social attitudes about handicap, particularly mental handicap.

Family Korner, Germany

In general we have found people supportive and accepting of John. Where there have been difficulties, it is usually due to a lack of experience or a lack of exposure to people with Down Syndrome.

Family Feighey, Ireland

"Very bad, if not worse than bad." This is due partly to the belief that childhood disability is due to parental alcoholism! Parents are ashamed of their handicapped children. "The mentality of our society is such that people are afraid of something that they don't know." Parents often deny the existence of a handicap.

Family Zelentsova, Russia

UNFAIR TREATMENT

There are many examples of the way social systems exclude and put obstacles in the way of people with mental handicap and their families. This form of discrimination and disadvantage often interacts with other forms of disadvantage related to race, class and gender.

My first daughter was a premature baby. The first blow was that she was a girl, which was a big disappointment. Added to that, she was underweight, and her eyes were hurt by the forceps.

Family Murthy, India

His mother had just separated from her ex husband, who is an Indian Muslim, when Alan was only three years old. Alan has a dark skin color. Sometimes the public mistake him for a Malay, which his grandparents and his mother were unable to accept initially. Indeed, they were not so much affected by his intellectual ability as by his appearance.

Mother actually overheard a shop owner calling Alan names because of his appearance, and he was very impatient with Alan

Family Yan, Singapore

When he was about 4 years old, his parents looked for a place in the University kindergarten. However, the Head refused to take Zhijia: "It is too difficult. We are a distinguished, nationally famous kindergarten and we have many distinguished visitors. We cannot accept your son!"

Family Song, China

As regards access to education, his parents sent him to nursery school when he was 10 years old. After staying there for 2 years he was sent to ordinary primary school where he was not accepted due to his intellectual disability. This is a common phenomenon in our country where mentally handicapped children are denied their right to education.

Family Mluki, Tanzania

Her parents sent Monti to school from the age of four. "We wanted to socialize her and to educate her." After a few months the teacher told them: "Your daughter is mentally handicapped. She has no brilliant career in her brain. She does not behave normally. Please take her away!"

Family Mamun, Bangladesh

Mohammed was never admitted to school and had no access to education until the last year at the MRB center which he now attends (aged 28).

Family Tareek, Lebanon

The teachers blamed the parents for their son's behavior problems (he was epileptic and mentally handicapped). They blamed the parents' "style of living," their "overprotection," their having only one child and their "lack of love."

"This made us very angry; it created our energy to change the situation!"

Family Ryo, Japan

The pediatrician told parents it was a waste of time for them to bring their son to the Institute and they should keep him at home.

Family Setty, India

After 13 years I suddenly found myself pregnant. I was then 42 years old... I had to go once a month to the maternity department, where I was not treated well at all. Before this pregnancy I had nine different pregnancies. Four were miscarriages. I was never so mistreated and humiliated then. This time I was mistreated because they thought I was too old to be pregnant. I used to feel ashamed of myself throughout my pregnancy... After Fatima was born, the pediatrician came to my bed to check on Fatima. I was holding her and he started almost yelling at me in front of all the others: "Why did you get pregnant, you, a 42-year-old lady? How did you get pregnant? Why weren't you put on contraception? Do you know your baby is very sick?"... I felt so humiliated and ashamed.

Fatima's Family, Jordan

The center felt that Susan was suitable for open employment and got her a fast-food restaurant job. Her colleagues bullied Susan and asked her to do their job as well.

Family Chan, Singapore

TAUNTING AND ABUSE

Ju Hun's teacher moved to a mainstream school and Ju Hun joined his class, but the other children did not accept him but teased him. So whenever the teacher was away from school Ju Hun stayed at home and refused to go to school.

Family Ha, Korea

What irks the parents most is the teasing of their daughter by street urchins and "lower class" persons.

Family Murthy, India

His grandmother suspected that the first maid whom they employed had "played with" Alan at home when there was no one around. According to the grandmother she once caught them fondling each other in the bedroom and giggling together.

Family Yan, Singapore

My mother-in-law put pressure on me to have more children, so I continued to bear one after the other, hoping for a normal child. The first six were all alike while my mother-in-law's [children] were normal. Her children began to mistreat and abuse my children.

Family Abdel-Kader Ayesh, Jordan

The school had very high academic standards and was rigid in its approach. The school used severe discipline. That led to Gaku's behavior problems, and he did not want to go back to school. Yes, he was hit in school, and that led to him having headaches and pains lasting up to three days.

Family Ryo, Japan

One time I saw a person with four or five handicapped children around him at the bus stop. He was showing them pornographic photographs to get his thrills of seeing them aroused.

Family Eed, Jordan

Mallory came home because of an abusive situation, and because of that the government of Nova Scotia was put into a position to provide us with financial support... Mallory received second-degree burns at her training center.

Family Horner, Canada

ADDITIONAL COSTS

It is a financial burden. Having two children is more expensive than one (families in China are allowed to have two children only if one child has a disability). A nurse is an additional cost also.

Family Song, China

Family life is more or less the same [with a disabled child] except that we have less money.

Family Leung, Hong Kong

At present all provision must be made by parents themselves, and this is only possible for the few that have the means to do so.

Family Chowdhury, Bangladesh

Professor Chowdhury turned down offers of banking jobs because of the pressure this would involve, and also refused work that might involve transfers which would dislocate the family.

Family Chowdhury, Bangladesh

I always took two village girls into my home so that they could play with my daughter, and they would stay for two or three years.

Family Salam, Bangladesh

I am worn out financially from all the presents I keep buying to bribe my neighbors' children to accept Lana.

Family Saleh, Jordan

My husband used to pay half his salary to the Association to pay for Ra'ad's care.

Family Eed, Jordan

The cost of medication is extremely high. Whatever I pay for Akrima is at the cost of his brothers and sisters. Sometimes I take a day's leave to take him to speech therapy, to the doctor's, or to find a placement for him... I pay half my salary for his tuition. I have spent 20 years working for the government, but I still don't have a car or a home.

Family Sarayra, Jordan

An insurance policy has been taken out for him.

Family Acuthan, Singapore

It was very expensive to engage a private tutor to teach Mui Poh.

Family Lee, Singapore

WHAT THE FAMILY MEMBERS WITH DISABILITIES CONTRIBUTE TO FAMILY LIFE

Most families express joy and pride in what family members with a disability contribute to the family both directly and indirectly. Parents and other relatives praise their strengths and abilities; their personal qualities and the contribution to family life that living with and caring for a person with disability brings.

Susan is a great help with the housework. With Susan around the house will be very tidy. She also used to help mother with babysitting her younger sister when she was a baby. Mrs. Chan said: "Life without her is something missing. She is even more helpful than her other sisters to me at home." Susan will help to sweep and mop the floor, tidy the rooms, fold the clothes and do many other things. Susan said she could wash clothes as well.

Family Chan, Singapore

Ju Hun brings a lot of happiness to the family. Ju Hun has brought me honors [prizes for the journal that his mother kept and had published].

Family Ha, Korea

Ghinwa and her sister have contributed so much to family life that the atmosphere at home is that of a family with very strong bonds.

Family Ghareb, Lebanon

Haifa spends her time when not at school visiting neighbors and family friends. She is extremely sociable and is liked by everyone. Haifa contributes happiness and open-mindedness to family life.

Family Hashem, Lebanon

The disabled person gives you the gift of loving and sharing. He taught us patience and the creation of a nice cozy atmosphere,

Family Osseirian, Lebanon

Since the story of Mervin was written, he developed a chest infection and died. His adopted family and friends are bereft. "The house will never be the same because he kept us all going. He was so funny with a lovely nature and he loved to tease us.

Family Griffin, New Zealand

His grandfather spoke of Zhijia's many strengths. He has an excellent memory for TV programs, advertisements, the weather forecast; he can speak a foreign language (English) and sign language. He is good at using equipment such as the video or tape recorder, telephone and electronic games. He is a very loving boy and writes letters to those he loves.

Family Song, China

Nahla helps me to take care of Ahmed when I am at work now. She now babysits for a 7 month baby with Down Syndrome whose mother is a teacher. She does a great job. When Hala finished her schooling she went to her uncle's home to help with the housework... Khadejeh comes to the centre every day to help out in the preschool class. She loves children. Nuhaila is in a vocational center and works in ceramics. She won first prize for her work on two ceramic pieces in an annual competition for creativity in Jordan

Family Abdel-Kader Ayesh, Jordan

He washes his own clothes, cleans the premises, does gardening, cuts grass for the goats and pigs' feed, weeds the banana plantation, and chops firewood for cooking.

Family Mlaki, Tanzania

Fortunately enough, she is very strong and hardworking, and she contributes a lot to the family in terms of unskilled work. She cleans the home, washes her own and her sisters' clothes, herds the cattle and goats, and does weeding and gardening together with her parents.

Family Maro, Tanzania

My daughter is an expert at housework.

Family Mamun, Bangladesh

She does tasks that could be boring for others but which seem to bring her satisfaction... She is proud of her salary.

Helen's Family, Belgium

Gradually the whole goal of achieving and making a place for yourself, the pressure seemed to dwindle away. My parents came to a realization that they were going to have a child that is not going to achieve in the same way. There was a big change in the dynamics of the whole family. Everyone was allowed to be the way they are. Positive change — an attitude to have the freedom and right to be the way they are and not be judged. Therefore, healthy attitudes began to form.

Family Cooke, Canada

You have many great gifts and talents, many of which I am just discovering. But two that you display so unselfishly are love and forgiveness. The world has not been particularly kind to you, but when the tumult is over you are always ready to give a big smile and get on with the day-to-day task of living.

Family, Canada

THE ROLES OF INDIVIDUAL FAMILY MEMBERS

Support from the extended family, where it exists, is a key factor in determining the quality of life of the family. Individual members play many important roles in the care of the disabled member and in supporting the whole family. There are, of course, many differences within and between families.

Mothers

Mothers typically remain the major carers throughout all the regions of the world, though there are a few rare exceptions. Many work hard to help their disabled children to learn and develop; to balance the needs of the child with mental handicap with the needs of their other children and of the family as a whole. Most do this remarkably well and grow in strength. But for some, at least, there is a significant cost.

Mother is the main person taking care of Mui Poh at home.
Family Lee, Singapore

As the housewife, the mother has to pay full attention to the child. There is no such restriction on other family members.

Family Basavaraj, India

His mother tried to stimulate Ju Hun and help him learn by herself. His father offered her no support.

Family Ha, Korea

Ahmed goes to work with me every day.

Mother, Family Ali, Jordan

My husband was working as a janitor in the court on a very low salary. His salary couldn't cover the cost of our living independently. I started to sell Kayk (a popular Arabic bread eaten for breakfast) to help bring in enough food for the children. Shortly after I moved to our independent home (away from Father's family), I gave birth to my seventh child, Samer. He is my only normal child. I knew this from the minute he was born. Four years later I had Ahmed, but he again was not normal. With Ahmed I had eight children to support... My husband needs someone to take care of him. He cannot look after the children.

Family Abdel-Kader Ayesh, Jordan

My wife is 28 years old. All day she is very busy with all the children, especially Akrima. He needs constant care and attention.

My wife was always much more tired than me. Sometimes she did not leave the house for 2 to 3 months.

Family Sarayra, Jordan

The mother is a very dynamic person who is skillful at taking good care of her family without the help of a maid, which is usual in Amman.

I used to give him a lot of my time to compensate for his

needs. ...It took a lot of work to get him to accept a daily bath. I trained him to eat properly.

Family Jarer, Jordan

I am the only one to take care of Lana from the beginning. I don't allow her father to help.

Mother, Family Saleh, Jordan

Momotaj Mamun [mother] was one of the three special teachers trained to teach children with learning difficulties in Jamalpur. Her first reaction was "I can't do it!" but Jowaherul [father] could find no one else, and she agreed when he insisted.

Family Mamun, Bangladesh

The family had poor accommodation at the time of the birth, as they were in transit, and shortly after Muna was born her father had to leave to go to Chittagong. He was away for four months... His wife was fragile and herself in poor health. The family had no support... The next few years he had to leave repeatedly, leaving his wife alone. She suffered from recurrent ill health and also from recurrent depression.

Family Hossain, Bangladesh

His parents commented that all through their lives they have been preoccupied with basic daily worries about Samuel and their duty to care for him, and that it is for this reason that his mother has not worked in her profession for many years but has stayed at home to care for and tend to the needs of her son

Samuel's Family, Israel

I feel I am weaker. I want to be there and help Mohammed, but I can't.

Mother, Family Accaur, Lebanon

I learned how to drive a car so that I could bring her to the private class. I started a degree in psychology and speech therapy so that I could help my daughter.

Mother, Helen's family, Belgium

I feel lucky and privileged to be able to stay at home full time, because I believe that supports that the family can offer are the most important for the welfare of all my children, including John.

Mother, Family Feighey, Ireland

I still find it hard to deal with. Support from school and family members is making me stronger and less embarrassed about Sa'ed.

Family Itani, Lebanon

Fathers

Many fathers take a supportive role and offer their wives emotional support in caring for their disabled child or adult family member. Only very rarely do they take a major role as carers themselves. The majority see their role as the traditional one of bread- winner and head of the family. There is some indi- cation that fathers, perhaps because they are less closely involved in the day-to-day care of their child, have greater difficulty in coming to terms with their child's disability; sometimes this took far longer for them, perhaps particularly where a son has mental handicap. Where fathers do take an equal or major role in caring, this is the most crucial source of sup- port to their wives.

His father offered her no support. He went fishing when he had time off work. She felt she accepted the fact that Ju Hun had a disability, but her husband found it harder... When his mother took Ju Hun to special school, she showed his father the children at school with worse conditions than Ju Hun. From that time he has accepted Ju Hun and his disability. Fathers in Korea do not play with their children or get so involved in their upbringing... During the conference which his mother attended, his father took Ju Hun to school and picked him up each day.

Family Ha, Korea

Muna's parents now live separately. His wife's physical health has improved, and although she still suffers from depression she does not want psychiatric treatment. She is unable to cope with Muna, who is now cared for by her father.

Family Hossain, Bangladesh

He needs help with feeding, and his father helps him daily with toileting, bathing and dressing. He is very attached to his father and frequently comes to his father for help. The most pressing worry is the lack of help when his father is not there.

Family Chowdhury, Bangladesh

Chitralekha is very fond of her father. She understands that all her needs are provided by her father.

Family Murthy, India

My husband has always helped with Ra'ad.

Family Eed, Jordan

Father is more accepting and cooperative.

Family Itani, Lebanon

My husband is a very compassionate person and understanding of what I am going through.

Family Saleh, Jordan

Father is more accepting. He is willing to learn and work hard to help Mohammed.

Family Accaur, Lebanon

His father often takes his son along on afternoon errands and on walks so that Samuel will get out of the house, since Samuel has no friends.

Samuel's Family, Israel

Grandparents

> *Grandparents often have a major role and influence. Some grandparents live with or near their children and grandchildren and are in a position to offer support on a regular, sometimes daily basis. Some live further away and may offer intermittent support or financial support. Of course, not all grandparents understand or are supportive. It is also clear that grandparents sometimes have their own agendas and occasionally add to the pressures and difficulties of the families.*

Grandmother, a homemaker in her late fifties, suspected that something was wrong about Alan's head when it was bigger than normal... "It was my mother who insisted that he should not have the operation as there was a possibility that he might be blind after this. I gave up and thought there was not much hope for him." But with much hope and refusing to listen to the doctors, grandmother persisted in feeding Alan "rice by rice" until he was able to take food... Alan was brought up under the care of his maternal grandmother since birth.

Family Yan, Singapore

Grandfather took the initiative in consulting many experts.

Family Song, China

Her parents-in-law were sympathetic and supportive (in spite of having kept from her that a distant relative of father also had Down Syndrome). Her own mother advised her to "Put her child away!"

Family Ha, Korea

Paternal grandmother is willing to look after Mui Poh for a short time.

Family Lee, Singapore

When the parents became aware of the disability of both the children, they got frustrated and blamed their fate. The father said it would be better to be childless than have such handicapped children. Mother has little hope of training the children. Maternal grandmother and maternal uncle look after the children well, but some of their relatives discourage the parents.

Family Kallianpur, India

Both the maternal and paternal grandparents are very cooperative and helpful. They helped a lot in identifying the delayed milestones.

Family Basavaraj, India

I left him once with my parents in Karak. They rushed to Amman in the middle of the night because he was ill and they didn't know how to cope with him. We seem to be the only ones who can deal with him. It is the same with the grandparents on my wife's side.

Family Sarayra, Jordan

Mazada Khaloon [mother] is the only daughter in her family, and they did give considerable support in helping to look after Abrare and in sharing the parents' feelings.

Family Chowdhury, Bangladesh

He was taught toilet training and feeding by his grandmother. The child was helped to live independently with both paternal and maternal grandparents.

Family Setty, India

My mother-in-law told the children about their brother.

Family Ali, Jordan

My mother has visited all the witchcraft liars to get a cure for my son.

Family Sarayra, Jordan

My mother-in-law still doesn't believe that there was anything wrong with Khalid.

Family Jarar, Jordan

His paternal grandmother told me that he was not a man and that I would have to have another brother for Jerias [non-disabled child].

Family Shakar, Jordan

In a letter to their daughter after she gave birth to a child with mental handicap, these grandparents wrote:

To see you confront your destiny with such strength and courage enabled us also to be strong. We fed ourselves with your courage and the example you and your husband gave us, remaining united to face the situation generated by your baby's physical limitations, our beloved grandson. You told us, "We must struggle for the most disadvantaged and work for those with the greatest needs." And this is how we all, your parents, your other son, your brothers and your husband's family form one single cell, one nucleus, one will; we are all with you.

Family, Mexico

My father [maternal grandfather] told us that we would run into experiences with Andrew that we would never have dreamed of in our lives. Some would be good and some not so good. He said that if you could come away with something good out of every experience then everything would be fine. We have really applied this to our lives, have made this our creed and tried to instill this in our children

Family Nish, Canada

Mother [maternal grandmother] was a very practical person. Apart from minding David, she might come in and do the dishes, make a casserole for dinner or all of these things — but there was moral support too. My father never accepted that David was brain-damaged, because David understood everything said to him. Dad thought that one day soon he's going to start to talk. Of course he hasn't started to talk.

David's Family, Australia

Brothers and Sisters

Brothers and sisters often play a key role. Parents often depend on them for practical emotional and social help with the child who has a disability. In their thinking about the future, parents often look to brothers and sisters to take on the caring role when parents are no longer able to continue them-

selves or after their deaths. But parents also ex-
press concern about their other children; often feel
sad or guilty that they did not give them the full
attention and care they might otherwise have had;
worry about their experiences. Brothers and sisters
themselves, like their parents, seem to have a vari-
ety of experiences and feelings. Many emphasize
the positive benefits, but some also share the ef-
fects of discrimination and negative social attitudes.

Initially the parents were very shocked and refused to accept that their daughter was disabled. However, one of the eldest sisters worked with handicapped children, and she was the key in making her parents accept the problem.

Family Hashem, Lebanon

Joyce can't show her feelings like we can, but she can show us when she's happy by giving us one of her big, beautiful smiles that affect everybody forever... I often wonder what is going on inside her mind... It was pretty tough for me because I had to babysit Joyce as well as my other younger sister.

Sister, Family Morrison, New Zealand

It was not possible for Paul's sisters to engage in any out-of-school activities, because his parents could not meet both Paul's needs and his sisters' needs.

Family Shepherd, Australia

Greg's brothers were confused and bewildered, unable to relate to Greg.

Family Offer, Australia

Both older brothers are good babysitters if their parents need one.

Family Lee, Singapore

Father sometimes feels that they have neglected the needs of their other children because of giving their full attention to Mui Poh. Her elder brother agreed.

Family Lee, Singapore

Ratna remembered very clearly that when her father was dying he said to her: "Take care of Dhanesh, don't bother your mother." From then on, she has never failed her father in fulfilling his wish.

This is a 24-hour business... There is not much freedom... Things have been tough for Ratna lately, especially when her mother was no longer around to help out.

Family Acuthan, Singapore

His sister Joo Lee was involved in the [language] program. She tried to copy the model of her parents to make her brother speak. She tried to reward him with a biscuit and got bitten in the process!

Family Lim, Singapore

Since her older and younger sisters did not ask about Susan's condition, the family did not talk about it... Her sisters invite friends over sometimes. When their friends see Susan her sisters will simply tell them that she is their sister.

Family Chan, Singapore

Both Dai and Aya love and accept Gaku and understand him well. Gaku helped care for them when they were little. Their parents always explained everything to them from a very early age and involved them in activities with their older brother.

The primary school which Dai and Aya attended started to establish links and integrated activities with a special school. At this stage, Dai and Aya were "leaders" because of their experience.

Family Ryo, Japan

Parents have not talked to Shuang [younger sister] about Down Syndrome and what it means, but when she was about 8 years old she began to realize that Zhijia is different from other children. She only refers to this rarely, usually when they are quarrelling.

Family Song, China

Il Hun [older brother] showed mixed reactions to Ju Hun, both jealousy and affection. One day when he was eight or nine (Koreans reckon age from the time of conception), Il Hun returned from school and asked his mother if Ju Hun was a twin. He had seen another child with Down Syndrome who was a twin. She decided it was time to explain to Il Hun. She told him that Ju Hun had been very ill and that this had affected him. Il Hun accepted this because he had a classmate who was autistic. Previously Il Hun had often got cross with Ju Hun when he misbehaved or could not do things like other children. He called him, "Fool, Dummy!" and got very upset. At other times he played with Ju Hun and could be very helpful to him.

His mother expressed concern that Il Hun's development too had been restricted by Ju Hun and that he might have developed "better" with a "normal" younger brother. She felt that Ju Hun had often disturbed Il Hun when he was studying. In Korea students have to work very hard to prepare for their college entrance exams, and Il Hun suffered academically.

Family Ha, Korea

His younger brother loved Lee Eun when he was little, and Lee Eun has always got on well with his younger brother, but as he has gotten older Sin Myong thinks that her younger son has suffered through having a disabled brother. He has expressed resentment that his parents did not have another healthy child to share the tasks and to help care for Lee Eun. He was upset and hurt because of the teasing and verbal abuse

that Lee Eun was exposed to, such as taunts of "Pablo (Idiot)!"
He was also reluctant to bring friends home.

Family Yang, Korea

It is unlikely that his older brother will later take care of Alan.
He has his own problems and cannot be bothered with his
brother's welfare.

Family Yan, Singapore

Only Samer developed normally. He loves his brothers and
sisters, but he wishes he had a brother to go with him to school.
His mother expressed the worry that Samer will have "a load
of responsibility of looking after his brothers and sisters. I feel
most of my energy is given to his brothers and sisters."

Family Abdel-Kader Ayesh, Jordan

Suhair was very understanding concerning her brother's disability. She insisted that her fiance sit with Ra'ad and bring his
family to get to know him. She was very sensitive to Ra'ad.
She was engaged once before she met her present husband
but broke it off because she sensed that he was concerned
about having handicapped children. She is very happy now
and invites Ra'ad once a month to go and stay with her.

Zaid is 14 years old and not at all patient with Ra'ad.
Ra'ad interferes in Zaid's affairs.

Family Eed, Jordan

Jowaherul [father] is not sure what support Monti's brothers
would offer. Monti was very happy when they were born and
has always got on quite well with them. Her brothers are quite
polite and gentle with their sister,

Family Mamun, Bangladesh

I am not so rich but I am not so poor. I will leave some prop-
erty for Rumana. My son is angry about this: he says he will

look after her without that. My other son also says he will look after her. But he is not married yet, and it depends on the wife in the family.

Family Salam, India

Jamie's younger sister, Jenny, seemed to be having a hard time dealing with some of Jamie's behaviors towards her. We really felt in many ways that Jenny was trying to mother Jamie, telling her exactly how, where and what to play.

Family Scattergood, United States

When Riley was six he lost his first tooth, and this was somewhat remarkable because this was about the first thing he had done "on time," developmentally speaking. Our daughter Sarah was extremely excited about the event and responded by saying how wonderful and terrific it was. I agreed... By dinner I had heard the proclamation of the event so many times that I really didn't care if Riley ever lost another tooth. Still, she continued with the same excitement as if the news had just broken... I agreed again... Sarah confronted my indifference by saying that I didn't seem very excited. I ... asked her if she had any idea of the implication this event might have? She admitted that no, she didn't really know. I explained that the deaf-blind tooth fairy was going to come. My husband picked up the tale. He went on to remind her that the deaf-blind tooth fairy had never been in our home and would probably be banging around for days. We would be lucky to get any sleep at all. Sarah was silent as the conversation continued in this manner. After a few moments she excused herself from the table... After about fifteen minutes Sarah returned with blood running down her cheek. ...She held up her own tooth between her fingers and announced, "Now the deaf-blind tooth fairy can have a sighted guide!"

Family Ford, United States

FRIENDS AND NEIGHBORS

The support that was available to families particularly in the locality where they lived was crucial in determining their quality of life.

The neighbors warned their children from associating with Jacqueline because she is violent and quarrelsome... No support whatsoever was received from the neighbors or the local community.

Family Maro, Tanzania

As regards the neighbors: some are sympathetic, others say that the family has given birth to a mad person or an imbecile. No support was received from neighbors and the local community, because the problem of mental retardation is not known to many people but is seen as an individual and family problem.

Family Mlaki, Tanzania

Our home is situated in the company flats. There is a total of 12 families living there. All the elders, children and their relatives know her almost from her birth. So she has been simply accepted. They treat her normally. The children try to play with her; the elders encourage her by listening to her, wondering at her achievements.

Family Murthy, India

Neighbors and their children used to help a great deal.

Family Setty, India,

I got lots of encouragement from my friends, who treated her as if she was normal. They used to encourage me in my work. One of my friends used even to look after my daughter when I had to go out for a short time... My friends' children used to play with her; teach her games; care for her. They used to get her share of sweets and food.

Family Murthy, India

In our old neighborhood the neighbors were nice. They would take Akrima into their homes. The present neighbors don't interact much. They are upset if we leave him outside.

Family Sarayra, Jordan

The neighbors and other people around us not only didn't accept him but attacked us.

Family Eed, Jordan

When Khalid was young they [neighbors] would look out for him and took really good care of him.

Family Jarer, Jordan

The neighbors had come to know about Mui Poh, as she used to scream at night when they first moved to this neighborhood three years ago. According to the parents, the neighbors are generally understanding and do not seem to be impatient towards them.

Family Lee, Singapore

Ratna and Dhanesh are very fortunate to live next door to a family whom she could rely on when she needs help. The whole family, from the grandmother to the young grandchild, help to keep an eye on Dhanesh whenever Ratna needs to attend to something urgently. They like Dhanesh and he likes them. Dhanesh has learned to respond to the old grandmother by calling her "A-ma" now.

Family Acuthan, Singapore

Neighbors often told Mrs. Chan that she is very fortunate to have Susan around... They described Susan as very "Houzui," which means being courteous enough to greet them every time she sees them. The neighbors liked Susan. Mrs. Chan looked pleased when she talked about this feedback.

Family Chan, Singapore

Our relationship with neighbors and the local community is very good. We have very caring, warm and supportive neighbors and friends... Ghinwa goes out to visit neighbors, relatives and friends.

The support we received from the neighbors and local services was overwhelming. They did not turn their back on us but welcomed Ghinwa with open arms and love.

Family Ghareb, Lebanon

Most of the family's relatives and friends sympathized but gave no support.

Family Chowdhury, Bangladesh

The family had no support from family and friends because they were in transit (Father was in the services).

Family Hossain, Bangladesh

The family have had good neighbors who accept Lee Eun and help to look after him.

Family Yang, Korea

The neighborhood where the family lives accepts Eu Jin and his disability well. Eu Jin participates in the activities of the residents' association. In the last neighborhood where they lived there were also very helpful residents. They helped to babysit Eu Jin and his sister.

Family Lim, Singapore

One day Andrew was determined to go outside and play. He opened the door and crawled out into the street. My neighbors must have thought I was a terrible parent for letting my child out on the street, but you know, I celebrated the fact that he opened the door on his own.

Family Nish, Canada

The family lives in an apartment building in Tel Aviv, but they have little social contact with their neighbors. They are rather solitary. The extended family is rather small, and there are very few family members with whom they are in touch.

Samuel's Family, Israel

It was a great shock to our families and friends when they learned about the handicap. But we have been very lucky, though, because every one came to visit us at the hospital. I thought that they might not have the courage to face us, but they had. So I did my best to talk about my child's handicap to help them feel at ease with me. Their friendship was so necessary to me, and I didn't want them to go away because they did not feel at ease.

Family Oleffe, Belgium

EFFECTS ON FAMILY LIFE

The majority of families with a member with mental handicap live in areas where there are few services and supports to the whole family. In most countries, discrimination toward disabled people and their families exists and continues. Many families tell of the tasks they have to undertake in caring for their disabled relative and, in the context of societal attitudes, what difference the experience of caring has made to them and to family life. A few say it has made no difference or little difference. Many families, nearly all, emphasize the benefits they have gained as well as the difficulties they have faced.

DIFFICULTIES AND RESTRICTIONS

There is not much freedom. If a friend happens to call and make an appointment on the same day I am unlikely to make it... Ratna was very open about sharing that she chooses not to marry as she thought that it would jeopardize the marriage as she will continue to take care of Dhanesh.

Family Acuthan, Singapore

Mrs. Chan could not remember any restrictions to family life in having Susan.

Family Chan, Singapore

Family life is more or less the same except that we have no money.

Family Yip, Hong Kong

His parents do not go out to participate in any social activity or perform any errand without Samuel.

Samuel's Family, Israel

If there is a disabled child in the family all the family need more energy, more patience and must pay greater attention to the child. The family have less time for themselves They must always join in activities with the disabled child but are not always in the mood.

Family Song, China

If I had imagined how difficult it would be I would have been frightened. You do not really understand until you are in the middle of it.

Family Deane, New Zealand

There is no restriction on anyone in the family as [she] is able to mix with other people... Other family members attend all religious and social functions within and outside the family.

Family Murthy, India

The effect of the disability on family life was devastating. There was total readjustment of the daily routine activities to suit the child's requirements. The activities of the parents were crippled. The disability of their son has caused deep mental trauma on his parents.

Family Mukund, India

It is difficult to go out on the spur of the moment, and every-thing has to be planned before any leisure activity can be pursued.

Family Ghareb, Lebanon

We surrendered ourselves to Mui Poh.

Family Lee, Singapore

I can never leave the children on their own, because I am afraid that Saed will hurt them or he will hurt himself because he is unaware of the dangers of daily life.

Family Itani, Lebanon

Muna's parents now live separately. His wife's physical health has improved, and although she still suffers from depression she does not want psychiatric treatment. She is unable to cope with Muna, who is now cared for by her father.

Family Hossain, Bangladesh

I have accepted the situation I am in, and I pray and fast and do what God orders me. I thank God for what he gave me, but so many times I feel *kahr* (helplessness with deep-rooted anger because of unjust treatment and humiliation). Why should all those around me be better off than I am? Every day when I walk to school and see six [handicapped children] walking in front of me, I cry. There are times when I play with them and enjoy doing things with them, but this feeling of *kahr* is in my heart. I try not to show it to my children, but the moments of sorrow are much more than the moments of hap-piness.

Family Abdel-Kader Ayesh, Jordan

Akrima was difficult from the day he was born. We couldn't get him to suck: he refused his mother's milk. We had to feed him by spoon for 6 months. When he did take his mother's breast, feeding him was still extremely difficult. Also, he wouldn't sleep. When he did sleep his sleep was shallow, easily disturbed by any movement. We couldn't get him to sleep for more than 2 hours.

We are exhausted and Akrima is difficult with his brothers and sisters. He always annoys them.

Family Sarayra, Jordan

The problems we may have are because we are both tired and tense and because of the lack of sleep at night for many days because we have to care for our daughter... I told him [husband] the other day that King Hussein gave pardon to all the prisoners in Jordan but my prison was not included.

Family Saleh, Jordan

We found out that Riley did not sleep at night. Ever. We also found out that we owed the various hospitals and ambulances about $300,000. I call this "rock bottom"... you see, I had lost my dream for my son.

Family Ford, United States

The whole family has to sacrifice and divide their time so that you can continue to have a harmonious life... When you have a disabled child it will change your whole life and personality.

Family Accaur, Lebanon

All families have their ups and downs.

Family Offer, Australia

All of Paul's family missed out on opportunities which are the normal province of families. That is, his cousins were not able to play with him because Paul did not play. His aunts and uncles were not able to interact either with Paul or with Paul's mother and father, because caring for Paul and interacting with the wider family were mutually exclusive activities. Paul's grandparents were unable to do much more than provide loving care — they were hard pressed to cope with the rigors of being responsible for Paul... As time passed, caring for Paul became too demanding for his grandmothers. When Paul's younger sisters were born, caring for them was tightly structured around Paul's needs and demands. Their care has always been incidental and provided on the basis of what was left over after Paul's demands were met.

Family Shepherd, Australia

BENEFITS AND GAINS

Nearly all families feel they have gained from their experience of living with a child or relative with disability. Some mention practical benefits of the help or contribution made by the disabled person to family life; many more greatly value them for the person they are. Most feel that they themselves have gained in personal development and strength.

Kristen has taught me an enormous amount about what life really means. She has been through so much hardship; she struggles so often to pull through adversity against incredible odds; she shows so much spirit and such a will to live that I cannot doubt that she has wanted to live.

Family Deane, New Zealand

I am the proud father of a disabled son. Now I am well known as the father of Abrare, and he is very well known.

Family Chowdhury, Bangladesh

Through my daughter I have learned about disability. I have

become a volunteer social worker and can work with professionals. I have become more human: my heart is more full of human love.

Family Mamun, Bangladesh

Our experience of their disabilities have brought the whole family closer together, and there is a solid bond.

Family Ghareb, Lebanon

There are many positives. Such children have a lot to teach us on how to live, how to add to our experience. They provide an additional dimension. It's not true that families with a handicapped child are more unhappy.

Family Zelentsova, Russia

Our philosophy has changed. I had little understanding for people with disabilities, weak people, people with social difficulties. This has changed. Now I have a better understanding.

Family Ryo, Japan

This child has brought more to our lives as a family than any other experience we could possibly have.

Family Nish, Canada

I learned to be assertive, and it gave me the drive to speak out on behalf of all families.

Family Scattergood, United States

It took me three years to dismantle my own handicap. Frederica herself made the best contribution, as her development was so unlike the negative image that the books had imprinted on me. ...I gained some understanding of attitudes, reflections and insights which helped me to understand the relationships between mothers of handicapped children and the handicap of the mothers themselves.

Family Korner, Germany

Lynne has changed Barbara [mother]. She is now more assertive and is not frightened of standing up to authority.

Lynne's Family, UK

I think in some ways I'm not disappointed because something really good has come out of Craig's disability... I've learned a hell of a lot and I'm getting so much pleasure out of Craig.

Craig's family, Australia

I like to think that I have become more compassionate and concerned, not just about the disabled but about everyone in the community who is disadvantaged. I would have to say that I was very selfish and brought up in a sheltered life in a middle-class family. I wasn't in touch with the world outside. I would like to think that I have a greater understanding of such things now. I have learned to sort out what is important in life. I am not worried about the color of my hair or my golf handicap or what detergent I use.

David's Family, Australia

Dhanesh has helped me tremendously in my faith.

Family Acthan, Singapore

We have learned to be patient and open-minded about the miseries of life, and offer what we can to support our two handicapped children and each other.

Family Ghareb, Lebanon

He has turned me into a strong person.

Family Jarar, Jordan

Mrs. Lee recalled herself as a person who used to be impatient and have high expectations of her children. Over the years she has learned to be less demanding and does not lose her temper as often — she is more patient now and emphasizes "trying your best" rather than results.

Family Lee, Singapore

You develop an enormous power and strength to give the disabled person his/her rights and develop him/her in all areas, to make him feel happy and be a positive person in life.

Family, USA

THINKING ABOUT THE FUTURE

All families think about the future. When children are young the family focuses on educational needs, the immediate future. As children reach school-leaving age, adolescence and young adulthood, families confront plans for adult living. Often at this time they compare their disabled child's future with those of non-disabled children. As parents themselves age and lose their capacity to provide care, they express concerns about the future care of their son or daughter.

It is time to re-evaluate our family dreams for our children; to create a vision of this person fully included in our families if we're going to attain inclusion in education, in the community and in the workplace.

Family Ford, USA

Our task now is to help Pierre leave home one day, as naturally as possible. Therefore we must try to have him taking part in discussions and decisions that concern him .It is important that he can express himself and make his own choices We must have high expectations related to his capabilities. And maybe one day he will ask to leave home, and he should be sure that he is always welcome.

Family Oleffe, Belgium

Two and a half years ago (when John was one) I outlined my expectations in the following way: I hoped that John would be treated as an equal citizen; I hoped that he would have as many choices as possible available to him; I hoped that he would be respected as an individual and not be categorized.

Family Feighey, Ireland

I see a future that holds much hope. My other two sons, Steven and Lindsay, are more open-minded about Greg's disability. My two daughters-in-law are very interested in Greg and his life.

Family Briggs Clark, Australia

Day and night I think about the future and what is going to happen. I had many children because I kept hoping to have normal children to help take care of the disabled ones, because the extended family never gives moral or financial support to me.

Family Abdel-Kader Ayesh, Jordan

My only worry is his future when we are gone. I know that his brothers are excellent with him, but I want him to have an independent life. I will build two apartments above our house soon. One will be for him, and the other we will rent out. The money from the rent will be to pay for Khalid's living expenses. Khalid is a very organized person. He goes to sleep on time, sets his alarm clock, gets up on his own and faithfully does his household duties. He can be independent. His mother and I are thinking seriously of letting him marry. I want my kids to have equal opportunities.

Family Jarar, Jordan

I wish Lana will die with dignity before I do, the way she lived with dignity.

Family Saleh, Jordan

The future? Ra'ad still soils himself when he gets scared. His problems will grow as he grows.

Family Eed, Jordan

I hope in the future Saed will become totally independent and achieve a vocational skill that will lead to employment.

Family Itani, Lebanon

I wish and hope that Mohammed will become normal in the future. His father just wants him to improve and be taken care of in the best way possible.

Family Accaur, Lebanon

Alhaj Kamal Uddin would like Simul to have a good education and to become qualified. He has been told that Simul will reach a level of skills education, but his father would still wish him to become qualified.

If this is not possible, then I will help him with money to become a business man with the help of a good manager and guide. If this is not possible, then I shall allow him to work with machines. He is an expert in sewing. My heart is always crying for this child.

Family Kamal Uddin, Bangladesh

We are concerned about the time when we are no longer able to care for Abrare... There are no support schemes. Professor Chowdhury is trying to organize a trust and home care, but this is still at the planning stage.

Family Chowdhury, Bangladesh

My daughter is an expert at housework. I think my daughter will be normal one day. She may not be literate or educated, but she is good at organizing, and she will be able to live and carry out conjugal duties and have children. She is interested in having a family and is not embarrassed about this. When she is about 25 or 30 years old we will arrange a marriage for her with a gentle polite boy. We will supervise the marriage and her care for the children, and later her children can look after her and offer support.

Family Mamun, Bangladesh

I do not think of a marriage for Rumana. I do not want to make her life too complicated. But she goes to some marriage parties, and she says "I will marry" and "It is beautiful!"

When I retire I can do things with Rumana at home; I can start a poultry farm; I can do block printing; I can take her on outings.

Family Salam, Bangladesh

Mother feels that it is crucial for Eu Jin to become independent. "When he is not dependent on others for his needs, he could be more of a help to whoever he is staying with than a liability."

Family Lim, Singapore

Susan is growing up. She asks me for lipstick and wants to have long hair... Mrs. Chan knew that it was unlikely that Susan would marry one day.

"I have started saving Susan's monthly income for her. This may help her when we are not around. I am afraid that she cannot count and that others may take advantage of her." Her mother was not sure if her sisters are able to look after her... She hopes that Susan can continue to be self-sufficient so that she may not need to depend on others too much in the future.

Family Chan, Singapore

There'll always be a need to ask someone to look after him.

Family Leung, Hong Kong

The family is planning to establish a simple business like Xerox or screen printing for the time when he has completed his education to the best possible level. They are looking for suitable training in these skills.

Family Setty, India

Only lately, after 22 years of coping with raising Samuel, his parents are beginning to think that the time has come to break out of the rigid structure of their lives and enable Samuel to go out of his home to learn to lead a more independent life.

Samuel's family, Israel

My son should be able to live independently or be cared for in a good place. At the moment they are in residential institutions, sometimes with elderly people, treated like prisoners.

Family Zelentsova, Russia

When Zhijia has finished his education he will be able to get work. He will receive vocational training and will be able to work in a factory or a shop doing a simple skilled job. The government have set up such factories.

Zhijia's IQ has been assessed at 76 now — it has risen considerably since he started at special school. He will be able to live independently with some help from friends and society.

Family Song, China

Later she will be taught tailoring as part of her profession, as suggested by her parents, so that she can be independent and self reliant in the future.

Family Maro, Tanzania

As regards our views about the future of our child as a family, we think it is our responsibility to take care of her by providing her with small projects such as gardening or poultry keep-

ing in order to earn a living. In addition, if our financial resources permit, we intend to build a small house for renting
which will provide her with a sure and stable source of income for the rest of her life, because there is no policy or law
in our country to protect the right of equal job opportunities
to people with mental handicap.

Family Marandu, Tanzania

FAMILIES EFFECTING CHANGE

Many families, and especially parents of older people with mental handicap, were pioneers in setting up facilities for disabled children and young adults or in motivating others to do so. They were educators of their families, neighborhood communities, friends and professionals in understanding disability issues and enabling them to relate appropriately to disabled people. They formed groups to support each other, to share experiences and learn from one another and to act as pressure groups to advocate for the rights of disabled people. The source of their strength and energy was of course their concern for their disabled child or relative, but also their frustration and anger at their treatment by others and by society as a whole.

The teachers blamed the parents for their son's behavior problems... This made us very angry; that created our energy to change the situation.

They approached the school governors and asked for special support for Gaku. Previously there were no special support systems.

Family Ryo, Japan

We are fighting to create a system. Today I can do things, not when I am old and dead.

Family Zelentsova, Russia

His mother prepared the teachers, introduced them to Ju Hun beforehand, and suggested how they could model behavior towards him so that he is not made fun of by the other students.

Family Ha, Korea

Lee Eun's teacher had a limited ability to help him learn. She had 15 pupils and few teaching materials... It was then that Sin Meong Yang [mother] set up a parents' support group in order to offer the teacher and the school some support and teaching materials. Her husband fully supported this venture. The group developed and provided support not only to the school but also to each other, and this family support group movement spread nationwide.

Family Yang, Korea

The parents were advised that there was no medical treatment. Shortly after this, together with a group of professionals, they started an educational program in Dhakar.

Family Chowdhury, Bangladesh

The professionals at SCEMBR advised the parents to place Monti in a special educational program in Dhakar which had hostel provision. Because they were unwilling for Monti to leave home, they were advised to set up a branch of the association in Jamalpur and to start a special educational program locally.

Jowaherul [father] called a meeting of parents with children with learning difficulties, professionals and administrators, explained the situation and proposed that a local special education program should be set up. A local ad hoc committee was set up, and the Dhakar association sent 2 counsellors and a volunteer...

Jowaherul publicized the opening of the special class. The people of Jamalpur had no knowledge of mental handicap... Mental retardation had to be explained, and information was circulated in all the media to help raise public awareness: "Big doctors are coming to help boys and girls to learn!" There were programs on the radio; in the news in local cinemas; speakers used microphones to attract attention in public places.

He [father] arranged meetings in their home for neighbors and members of the community to explain about mental retardation to them. They now understand a lot about it.

Family Mamun, Bangladesh

The parents of several such disabled children have formed a self-help group, and we are trying to help each other in a small way.

Family Murthy, India

In the year 1987 the parents who used to attend speech therapy at AIISH formed a self-help group under the name Swasahaya Samuchhaya. They used to meet every Sunday on the lawns of the AIISH Institute and play with the children.

The parents used to play with children of other parents. This helped the children to mingle with others and reduced their hyperactivity. During these meetings the parents used to discuss various methods to train their children. The group as a whole gave great confidence to the parents to teach their children, and the group has now become one big family who all help one another.

Later the association felt the need for integrated education to encourage mixing with normal children, and the association succeeded in convincing a local primary school to open an integrated section called Sahana in 1987.

Family Setty, India

At times I find that when they stare too long, I would ask "Can I help you?" Then they would turn away.

Family Lim, Singapore

Being a teacher helps the mother to cope... "Well, I tried many approaches, some successful, some not so." All approaches involved Eu Jin and his sister at the same time. ...One method worked very well, and mother has actually put it together in a book entitled "Teach Your Child." It is a book for parents on how they can spend more "quality time" with their children with the creative use of a tape recorder.

Family Lim, Singapore

We have given our time and effort to start such a [comprehensive] program, but the government will not give us any support. As voluntary workers we can hire a limited number of teachers, but they are difficult to educate and train because of our budget.

Family Eed, Jordan

One doctor interfered and suggested that both Fatima and I be given vitamins to make us strong — the joke was that I could have more children. I got so angry that I stood up and started to lecture the doctors and doctors to be. I said it is true that I am a simple woman, but my eldest son is studying to be a pharmacist and another to be a hotel manager. I understood their joke and the sarcastic remarks. I told them that I had had enough of them. I said, "I have a question for you. Can any of you guarantee that you will not have a child like mine? I am satisfied with my child and what Allah gave me, but I have had enough humiliation and mistreatment." I said to the doctor who made the joke, "I hope you have a child like mine so you will learn to respect other people's feelings and stop this humiliation and mistreatment, especially of the mothers."

Fatima's Family, Jordan

I have met with people in the Ministries of Development and Health, schools for the deaf and centers for the mentally handi-capped.

Family Sarayra, Jordan

There were few centers in Amman, and none would accept her because she was a very difficult case. In 1978 a National Society for Mentally Handicapped Children was formed, and we started a center. It was myself and some other parents who had mentally handicapped children who were not taken by the available centers who formed the group. There was no one to support us.

Family Saleh, Jordan

Kristen's exclusion from school was the motivating force for her father to become President of IHC, to work together with parents and colleagues to persuade the government to amend the Education Act to include all children, including those with disabilities and intellectual handicaps.

Family Deane, New Zealand

In the meantime things were changing, thanks to brave and imaginative parents. Classes for special education were start-ing, and one started a workshop in her own house. It was a real relief for us that Helen found a place in this workshop after her years at school.

Helen's family, Belgium

I became very active in seeking this goal – living together and learning together from the kindergarten to the workplace – I began to work with Lebenshilfe in the Hamburg society "Par-ents for Integration."

Family Korner, Germany

I have reached burnout myself on committees... So much

committee work is about crashing into brick walls over and over again until you get a chink in the mortar... I had to be involved as it was the only way I was going to get Annie a place to live — my fight for survival.

One of the things we have done, and one of the reasons why our model is so radical at the time, was that we insisted on getting away from the traditional houseparent/helper model; we refused to hire Hospital Employees' Federation staff because their staff models are not based on client needs.

Annie's Family, Australia

I learned that families are the force, power and energy behind system change.

Family Ford, USA

FAMILIES' EXPERIENCES WITH PROFESSIONALS

Throughout the lifetime of a disabled person, the family are likely to come into contact with a variety of professionals. Many parents and family members tell of one professional or another who treated them and their disabled relative respectfully and humanely and who gave significant help and advice. Families are enormously appreciative of such professional support. Even more common, however, are accounts of inadequate information, lack of practical help or advice, and worst of all, insensitive or frankly oppressive treatment.

They visited a number of specialists and were given different answers and different treatments.

Family Mamun, Bangladesh

The head teacher refused to accept Zhijia (in kindergarten). "We are a nationally known kindergarten with many distinguished visitors. We cannot take your son!"

Zhya's father praised his teachers for their help. They were very kind and patient and taught him many basic skills.

Family Song, China

One senior teacher told him [father] that Muna would learn nothing, but he disagreed: "She may not learn in your way!"

He regrets that the relationship between parents and teachers is not good.

Family Hossain, Bangladesh

The teachers blamed the parents: their style of life, their having only one child and their "lack of love."

Family Ryo, Japan

Dulcie, a community worker, noticed that unlike the others [in the IHC family home], there were no family photos on the wall of Mervin's bedroom. She set about finding his family and including him in hers.

Mervin's family, New Zealand

Staff from Paul's former school and from his hostel were involved in planning meetings designed to develop a system of support for Paul that would succeed. Some people gave their time voluntarily; the school freed up Paul's ex-teacher by putting a relief teacher in place, and hostel staff were rostered to be able to attend... A new support worker was chosen and the work experience began. Within three days it became apparent that the new arrangements were going to succeed and by mutual agreement with all parties, including the family.

Family Shepherd, Australia

The doctor explained about Down Syndrome. He told the parents to prepare for the fact that even when he became an adult Ju Hun might not be able to live independently or be continent. He gave the parents no advice.

Family Ha, Korea

Ra'ad was in hospital for 2 months and both doctors gave him excellent care.

Family Eed, Jordan

I think the police need to be fully informed because they do not know what mental handicap is.

Family Eed, Jordan

After Fatima was born the pediatrician came up to my bed to check on Fatima. I was holding her and he almost yelled at me, "Why did you get pregnant — you, a 42-year-old lady? Why did you not use contraceptives? Don't you know that your baby is very sick? Today you will go home but you must bring her back to see me in 10 days' time!"

A year later when Fatima was in hospital again with a chest infection, two days later I was sitting by Fatima's bed, and the consultant pediatrician walked into the children's ward with a group of doctors on their morning round. He was a high-ranking officer, which was obvious from all the red colors round his neck and shoulders, and he was carrying the special Marshal's stick. He walked proudly in front of the other doctors. He came to me and took Fatima's chart and read it. He didn't look at Fatima. One of the doctors who treated Fatima spoke to him in English. After he was told the cause he never once looked at Fatima. He merely looked at me and scolded me severely. "Do you know this baby is very ill? Why do you bear children when you are so old? Your child is drastically underweight. She will never grow any taller or fatter. She will never learn anything in the future, Why did you ever get pregnant?" I answered him, "I thank Allah for what he gave me." I started to cry. Everyone was looking at me. I felt so humiliated and ashamed.

Then a woman doctor approached me and asked the other doctors if she could handle my case. She would supervise the baby and I wouldn't need to see anyone else in the hospital. She comforted me and told me that she herself had a mentally retarded son. Since then I only go to see her. I refused to see any other doctors.

Fatima's family, Jordan

I worried about the pregnancy because I was very tired, and I approached a few doctors for an abortion, with the encouragement of my husband. None would give me an abortion... It was an early delivery by Caesarean, like the other four. The doctor told my husband that the baby had many deformities and in a few hours he would swell up and die....

The headmistress and some of the others that I work with came to see me. Their visit was only a relief for me. They told the nurses not to let in any visitors and to give me something to let me sleep They also requested that I be able to hold my baby.

Family Ali, Jordan

When her condition got worse we took her to a gland specialist in Lebanon. In both places we were told that I was killing her with the amount of medication I was giving her.

Family Saleh, Jordan

The university graduates have their heads stuffed with theory that has nothing to do with reality. They study special education only because they have low marks and are not allowed to specialize in anything else. There are no good training programs. Those who come with degrees from abroad can offer only their degrees and nothing else. The media is inadequate; the Ministry of Education and the police don't do enough.

Family Saleh, Jordan

The family has seen many doctors and visited many places of help over the past seven years. Mrs. Lee was rather upset when the person in charge of their case kept changing due to unforeseen circumstances. They felt a lack of continuity in the service provided to them. They had to repeat themselves very often, and their problems could not be addressed immediately as it was always at the investigatory stage.

Family Lee, Singapore

The doctor should have told me more.

Family Leung, Hong Kong

Frederica was not born mentally handicapped because of her condition of Trisomy 21, but would become handicapped in the course of her development. She would have to be compared with other children of her age. It is against this yardstick that her intellectual development became apparent. It is we who experience her condition as a handicap.

All this only became apparent to me much later. The doctor was talking to me shortly after her birth about a "mutation," and the geneticist later used the word "Down Syndrome." I automatically took the traditional view: Frederica was born as a handicapped child...

The remedial gymnast who did exercises with Frederica three times a week at first gave me a lot of support and helped me to develop a more positive attitude towards handicap.

Family Korner, Germany

Riley made it during those first crucial hours and days, and after about a month we received a call from one of the nurses at the hospital who informed us that Riley was being "a bad boy" ...Once we arrived we learned that being a bad boy meant that Riley was not oxygenating. The doctor recommended discontinuation of life support, and the question they had for us was to decide if we wanted to hold our son while he died.

This was perhaps my introduction to advocacy. I was so angry that they had given up on Riley after he had fought so hard, and I was outraged that they could be so insensitive to us and our needs.

Family Ford, USA

Because she was not developing well she had many tests at her local clinic, but the staff told Barbara nothing except that her development was slow, and they added that she would catch up... When she challenged the clinic staff as to why she hadn't been told [that Lynne would never catch up], they replied that they did not want to worry her!

Lynne's family, UK

The department of mental health and mental retardation in our state had started a program where they paid an assistant of the parents' choice to go with the child to an integrated summer program... The special education teacher we hired sat down with the class the second day Elisabeth was there and explained that Elisabeth had a disability but that she was just like the rest of them: she had a home, a pet and her own room.

Family Carroll, USA

A doctor received us and told us with great simplicity, which revealed his humanism and his understanding of our situation; he let us see the great advantages of an intervention. He avoided speaking about the problems I would have later. He told us that life had to be lived day by day and that we should not worry about what would happen to me in the distant future. He helped us to understand that whatever difficulties we would face in the future could not be compared to the satisfactions we would have. How right he was!

Family, Mexico

The local council home help carers are very good, but the administration has been most unsatisfactory in recent years. They have tried very hard to limit their service.

David's family, Australia

I found that most of the time the health centers had no idea about disability. There are no pamphlets on disabilities given out to parents. The lack of information is terrible.

Marcus' family, Australia

They weren't concerned because there was nothing medically wrong with him, and they just wrote him off.

It wasn't until the cerebral palsy specialist came and spoke to us that we could really understand what cerebral palsy was... The doctors weren't sympathetic at all. They just said it can't get any worse than what we've told you. It was like talking to a box or something. They had no personal touch at all.

Craig's family, Australia

I soon got the help of a psychologist who did listen to me and answered my questions, questions doctors couldn't answer, questions not to be found in books. That was reassuring

Family Oleffe, Belgium

According to psychoanalytical theory, I was responsible for [my child's] handicap. He was a beautiful two-year-old child who didn't speak, showed no trace of emotion in his eyes, appeared to be deaf and walked on tiptoes. Primary autism was mentioned. In 1982 the media were discussing a recent scientific discovery concerning the fragile-x syndrome. This genetic defect can lead to an autistic syndrome. ...I did not feel accused any more.

How wrong I was! I still didn't escape psychiatric investigations. In 1985 I wanted my son to visit the day care center of a psychiatric hospital in Brussels; the psychoanalyst imposed psychotherapy on me.

I wonder how can a talking therapy repair a chromosomal defect? I didn't follow her advice.

Family, Belgium

It was with much trepidation that we went to the elementary school for parent-teacher interviews... Seated round the table were Rashaad's classroom teacher, his special education coordinator and a student teacher. We exchanged pleasantries, and before I could say a word, his teacher spoke. "The first thing I want to tell you is how much I have learned by Rashaad being in my class." He pointed to the wall behind us. "In fact," he said, "I now have a sign up there — I only wish all my students realize how much they have learned." We turned around. The sign on the wall read *The only handicap is a bad attitude*. Tears filled my eyes as we stunned just looked at the group of teachers.

He went on to tell us how amazed and impressed they all were by the sheer determination and motivation Rashaad displays and how willing he is to try everything...

The interview was like a breath of fresh air. It was for me the feeling of elation — of being finally understood and on side together.

Family Sayeed, Canada

FAMILIES' IDEAS FOR IMPROVEMENT

Families' experiences over time with a variety of services and professionals give them invaluable knowledge of what is wrong and where the gaps are in the supports to families with a member with mental handicap. They know most about their own and perhaps other families needs at various stages in the family life cycle and many families have important, constructive ideas for the future development of services to support families.

Preventive measures could/should be taken to prevent serious infections caused by mosquito bites by using prophylaxis such as comaquine, malariaquine or chloroquine or by using mosquito nets.

Family Marandu, Tanzania

We have tried to do typical things with Andrew. making sure that the rest of the family have their needs seen to as well. We try not to single Andrew out but rather treat him like everyone else in the family... Looking at the positive things and celebrating the little things.

Family Nish, Canada

What would help now are special training centers where a disabled person could be well trained in a certain field and have a proper job. They should be accepted in factories and banks and have other jobs, like other people with some more consideration. There should be more places for sports, sports training and leisure activities.

Family Osseiran, Lebanon

As advocates we must ask for more than mere tolerance for Jim in society. It is as important for Jim to be a friend as it is for him to have them.

Family Schweier, Canada

People with mental handicaps who want to get married or whatever need love and support from both sides of their family. Social services and welfare people make a lot of decisions about who can raise kids even before we get a chance to show we can be fit parents. Maybe we need a little help. But I'd like to challenge the public to tell any person with special needs that they can't have a child. They should have to prove you can't instead of just deciding that even before a baby is born and then taking it away. Sure there are people with handicaps who aren't great parents, but there are a lot of regular people who are bad parents. There are even rich people with lots of schooling, educated people, who are not good parents. But people with handicaps get singled out... Scott [son] has been an inspiration to me and has helped me with "People First." Before I go talk at a conference I get a little uptight and nervous. He always says "Go for it, Dad. You can do it and I"m proud of you!"

Family Mercer, Canada

Education of the public is the most important priority.

Family Pang, Hong Kong

She [Mrs. Chan] feels it would be better if there is more information and teaching for parents from the very beginning to help them plan for their child's future.

Family Chan, Singapore

If a handicapped child is born, the family should immediately investigate the causes to avoid having more handicapped children in the future. You have to teach handicapped children to care for themselves from an early age to avoid bigger problems later. Doctors must learn how to treat parents and that they have no right to humiliate them

Fatima's Family, Jordan

My hope is that there will be more integrated programs in the normal school systems so Ahmed will have the opportunity to benefit from his education in a normal way.

Family Ali, Jordan

The government, instead of having them [people with mental handicap] institutionalized, should give me support and I will care for them and teach them how to take care of themselves.

Family Abdel-Kader Ayesh, Jordan

There are many services, but they are scattered and provide mostly temporary help. There is no continuity plan for many of the available centers. The government must take responsibility for caring for children like Akrima [who is autistic].

Family Sarayra, Jordan

Families must be individually assessed and supported in ways that do not in themselves add extra pressure to the family. Siblings do have the right to some quality time. Respite in the form of vacation and after-school care, as well as out-of-home residential respite, are essential to ensure that families are able to operate somewhat normally sometimes. Without that opportunity, such families as mine develop along a path which is emotionally unsound, experientially deprived and ultimately unhealthy.

Family Shepherd, Australia

We wish we had known when Pierre was born what we know now: that a Mongoloid child is a child as a whole, and that to live with a disabled child brings changes to one's life but doesn't prevent the family from being happy.

In the future:
— we should try to get him known by others as much as possible so that he is considered as a person and no longer as a disabled person.
— to keep our energy and dynamism to create parent groups who can provide the opportunity to discuss, express their experiences of life and be together to try to solve problems and to develop friendship.
— we should not expect help from others or from the state. Instead we must get up and go and believe that we can achieve something together with other parents and professionals. With that strength we can try to obtain from national authorities what is due to our children.

Family Oleffe, Belgium

There are a lot of different services provided for John, some through the Special Care System and some through the normal system. I would suggest that the combination of the two is disjointed and disorientating. If there was one integrated system it would make more sense and be more wholesome in the fullest meaning of that word. It would also be less demanding on me and on John.

Family Feighey, Ireland

The trust and simplicity of Frederica's relationship with young children of her own age seemed to provide an opportunity to prevent the development of prejudice against handicap or at least to weaken it... This means living together and learning together from kindergarten to the workplace.

Family Korner, Germany

Respond to us. Inform us. Teach us. Include us.

Family Ford, USA

The state should help by providing pensions for disabled children; subsidies for medicine, telephones etc. Services should be directed to parents, not children

Family Zelentsova, Russia

Information about Down Syndrome should be available for all parents and families with a member with such mental handicap.

Support systems for families are only just beginning in Korea and must be developed.

Parents need counselling, knowledge and training in how to help their children. At present in Korea only trained teachers can teach children but those who understand their children best are parents. Parents need training to help their children, especially fathers. Mothers get more opportunities for this.

Family Ha, Korea

I must emphasize the importance of accepting disabled people as they are and of working to teach them... in basic self care and living skills which are all important at home and at school. Each school must have a kitchen and a bathroom so that this training can be given.

Family Yang, Korea

Violence in special education is a great problem There is no law against this in Japan. The lawyers in our association are working to change this.

What we want for our son and other people with mental handicap:
— The opportunity to get paid work and support
— The opportunity to live in a group home or an apartment independently
— The opportunity to marry if possible
— The opportunity to improve environmental conditions
More information is needed.

Family Ryo, Japan

Bangladesh is the poorest among the poor. Our government is lagging behind in offering support to families with a disabled member. We are trying to develop all services. Our literacy rate is a mere 24%. We can't do enough for our normal children. No one takes responsibility for disabled children. We do now have compulsory primary education but disabled children are excluded.

It's the same in the field of job opportunities; there is no scope for mentally retarded people.

Priority needs include:

• Support for families, including financial support. At present all provision must be made by parents themselves, and this is only possible for the few that have the means. There should be funding, especially for poor families.

• A level of education and a special curriculum that at least provides training in independent living and self care.

• The State should provide a center to care for the children with the most severe problems in collaboration with their families.

• Families should have control of services.

Family Chowdhury, Bangladesh

There are many obstacles in the path of progress and there is no social welfare in our country yet... I want to introduce a support system for families within the SCEMR [Society for

Care and Education of the Mentally Retarded, of which father is secretary general]

Family Hossain, Bangladesh

If I was asked to give advice to other parents in similar situations I would tell them not to give up, to treat their kids normally and to involve them in things that are normal. I think it is very important that they are in a normal atmosphere... I would just tell other parents to keep going and don't give up.

Craig's family, Australia

CONCLUSIONS AND IMPLICATIONS

These statements by family members and the stories as a whole are a rich source of relevant information. They give us an insight into the day to day experience of families with a member with learning disabilities and into the impact on family life of living and caring for a disabled member in the social context of the last years of the twentieth century.

We can learn much about our world and its values and its social systems from what families tell us and what they say also gives us powerful messages about how services to support families need to be organized and delivered and the ways in which professionals should work with families in order to ensure most benefit to disabled people and their families.

From the stage of diagnosis of an impairment, family members appreciate and derive benefit from the following:

- Honesty and a sharing of knowledge with both parents
- An approach that acknowledges and is sensitive to family members' feelings
- An informed, balanced account of what the future may hold, emphasizing the full range of possibilities and the difficulty of accurate prediction
- Sustaining hope and optimism by acknowledging the positives in living with and caring for a disabled family member
- Accurate, up to date information about relevant organizations, facilities and programs and about the legal rights of disabled people and their carers
- Genetic counselling

- A point of contact for further information and/or support
- Practical advice relating to the care and development of the disabled child or adult
- Respect and consideration for the disabled child or adult, as well as for other family members.

The themes of respect, acknowledgment of strengths, abilities and the contributions of disabled people and of their families and their need for clear, full, accurate and honest knowledge and information recur throughout the stories and are not limited to poorer families or developing countries. They are pleas from all families, old and young, rich and poor, highly educated or illiterate.

However, the stories do illustrate individual differences between families and also between individual members within families. The implications for professionals and organizations that offer services to families therefore include that such services should:

- Be individually tailored to meet the needs of each unique family
- Include a range of options, including emotional as well as practical supports
- Include all members who take part in day to day family life
- Support and enable family members to express their feelings, views and wishes
- Ensure that the individual needs of all family members are considered and balanced as far as is possible
- Remain flexible and appropriate to the stage of the family life cycle.

It is very clear from what families tell us that, while each family has its own unique characteristics, values, strengths and abilities, the family's experience is equally, if not even more potently, affected by the social context in which the family lives. The attitudes and behavior of the local community, the existence of social support networks as well as local services and facilities, all profoundly affect the quality of life of the disabled child or adult and their family.

Although there are marked differences between the extent and level of services in different parts of the world and, on a smaller scale, between different local areas, all the stories bear witness to universal discrimination and inequality.

All families struggle for information, services, facilities and practical advice. All families experience social discrimination in the attitudes of some members of the public and of some professionals. They experience exclusion from mainstream education, employment, accommodation, family activities, even insurance schemes. Discrimination in relation to disability interacts with other discriminations in relation to gender, race, sexuality.

It is no longer enough therefore for services to focus entirely on individuals or individual families. The families themselves regard social change as the key priority. Professionals, services and organizations responsible for them must increasingly adopt a broader approach, that is, one that includes:

- Advocacy
- Representation to policy makers in all fields
- Public education which supports and works alongside disabled people and their families in their struggle for equal opportunities and equal rights.

Families themselves have always been prime movers in this struggle. They have frequently initiated essential services and facilities. They raise public awareness of disability issues by educating their families, friends, neighbors and local communities. They establish organizations to support each other. Many develop enormous strength, creativity, resourcefulness and determination.

Professionals and services have a responsibility to:

- Acknowledge and give credit to families and individual members for their qualities, strengths and abilities and for their contribution to the care and development of the

person with disabilities as well as of the whole family
- Work in partnership with families, acknowledging the areas of their expertise
- Learn from, as well as with, family members, including through joint training programs
- Empower families, their individual members and their disabled members to develop and retain control over their lives.

We must all acknowledge that none of this is easy or simple. Changing social attitudes and systems is a long and arduous undertaking. Balancing the needs of the most vulnerable members of society and of families with all others is complex. Where there are conflicts of interest, as there inevitably are, independent advocates for the child or adult with learning disabilities will be needed, whether from within or external to the family.

For too long disabled children and adults have been discounted, excluded, abused and oppressed. The challenge of the 21st century will be to support them and their families to make their voices heard and to claim their equal rights.

BIOGRAPHICAL NOTE

Helle Mittler is co-chair of the Task Force on the International Year of the Family established by the International League of Societies for Persons with Mental Handicap. She is the parent of a son with cerebral palsy. After studying English at Cambridge University and bringing up her family, she taught in a secondary school and then trained and worked as a social worker and later as a psychiatric social worker in the Manchester Child Guidance Services. She now works as a staff development officer for Stockport Social Services Division, concerned mainly with child protection, family placement and disability issues. She has undertaken research into parental involvement in special education and more recently on the participation of family members in child protection meetings. She has travelled widely and also interviewed a number of the families whose stories are reported in this book.